**THE POWER
BEHIND
YOUR DREAMS**

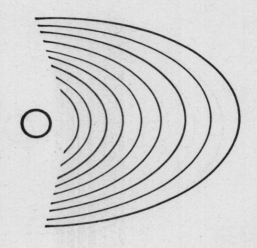

THE POWER BEHIND

 AN ESSANDESS SPECIAL EDITION • NEW YORK

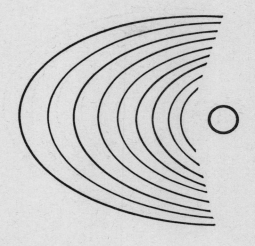

YOUR DREAMS

BETH BROWN

MACFADDEN-BARTELL · NEW YORK

To Bea Moore
for wisdom of the dream

THE POWER BEHIND YOUR DREAMS
SBN: 671-10549-3

Printed in the U.S.A.
Designed by Judith C. Allan

Chapter 1

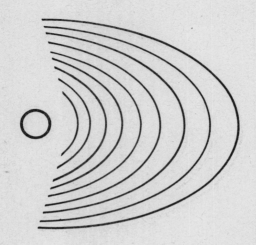

He that keepeth thee will not slumber. Behold, he that keepeth Israel shall neither slumber nor sleep.

—Psalms 121:3-4

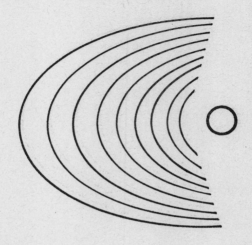

MARK TWAIN HAD A DREAM.

He dreamed that he saw the corpse of his brother Henry, arrayed all in black, lying in a metal coffin with a spray of dazzling white flowers across his chest like a decoration of honor.

Mark Twain drew closer to make sure it was Henry. His brother had been alive and well only a few days ago. Now as his gaze rested on the corpse, he noticed the single red rose set in the center of the spray. He touched it. He could almost smell it. Then he drew away from the casket and the dead man faded from view.

But the dream was so vivid that he told his sister about it when he woke up the next morning. Then he dismissed it as being nothing more than a dream.

After all, he assured himself, he had waved goodbye to his brother just before he boarded the Mississippi steamboat upon which he had signed, working up and down the Mississippi in his job as steersman.

Henry, too, had signed up on the *Pennsylvania,* a rival river boat. They had parted from each other with a laughing pact to meet each other in Memphis.

However, when Mark Twain reached town, he found it buzzing with excitement. It appeared that the *Pennsylvania* had blown up. All hands aboard had met death or been seriously injured.

Mark Twain boarded the vessel to search for his brother. He finally found him. Henry was in bad shape and was taken to the hospital. Here Mark Twain nursed him, day and night, going without either food or sleep.

But it was no use. In spite of all his efforts, his brother died without regaining consciousness.

Mark Twain collapsed from exhaustion. He

fell into a deep, uneasy sleep. When he awoke, he gathered up his strength to visit the mortuary.

Here—in grim formation—laid out on wooden slabs—were the silent figures of the men who had perished on the *Pennsylvania*. Henry's was the only body reposing in state in a metal coffin. It developed that his handsome young brother had won the hearts of the women in Memphis. It was their donation that had paid for the coffin. Mark Twain was moved beyond words by this generous gesture.

However, this was not all to the drama. As he stood there, solemnly regarding the corpse, he was startled to see a lady walking into the mortuary, carrying a small bouquet of white flowers. She placed the bouquet in all reverence upon the dead body.

It was then Mark Twain saw the finishing touch—that red rose in the center of the spray, conforming to the final detail in the dream he had experienced only a short time ago.

This was not the only dream of precognition in which the future revealed itself to Mark Twain. Time often turned the pages for him to read ahead what was to come. The story behind the inspiration for *The Great Bonanza* was another instance in which he dreamed the theme for the book which came to be written later on, just as he had envisioned it.

Dreams—too varied even to classify—have influenced mankind from the beginning of time.

Mozart, the celebrated composer, dreamed his finest compositions.

Voltaire sought and found the underlying themes for his poems when he was deep in sleep. He wrote them down upon awakening, preserving them for posterity.

Benjamin Franklin, while serving as Ambassador for America, would wait until he was tucked warm and snug in a featherbed, to meet and solve the crisis of the day behind as well as the one that lay ahead.

Both Thomas Edison—in business—and Harry S. Truman—as President of the United States—when baffled by a problem—would excuse themselves and leave the conference table, no matter who was present at the meeting, retiring to refresh themselves with a short nap. In reality, they used the few precious moments of recess to harness up their subconscious, fully expecting it to meet the problem. It never failed to deliver the solution, seemingly by magic, as if drawn out of thin air.

Men of note have often found fulfillment in their dreams, reaching while deep in sleep, the most difficult decision which eluded them while they were awake.

One of these instances involved Kekulé, the German scientist.

It seemed he was hard at work on a chemical project. The task seemed so intricate, the subject so elusive. Finally, he fell asleep. In a dream, he was shown the concept of the ben-

zene ring, the idea which has since revolution-
ized organic chemistry. He saw the atoms in
every detail—as they appeared before him—
and upon awakening, he immediately recorded
the hypothesis which came as reward to his
apparently hopeless search.

The Devil's Sonata, written by the well-
known violinist, Tartini, was inspired by a
dream. It is said that Tartini was struggling to
compose the melody but not a note would
come. Then he fell asleep and dreamed he saw
the devil appearing before him. The apparition
went to work. It snatched the violin out of Tartini's hand, tuned up the instrument, placed it
in position, and began to play the famous sonata which had been so elusive.

Tartini awoke and transcribed it, bar upon
bar. He gave it the appropriate name of *The
Devil's Sonata.* His sleeping dream proved lu-
crative beyond his wildest waking dreams. It
brought him fame and fortune.

Many a celebrated mathematician has solved
a complex problem while deep in sleep.

Condorcet was one of these, wresting an answer in a single night to a question that had
baffled him for many months while he was
awake.

Coleridge wrote *Kubla Khan* through the in-
spiring aid of a dream. He had been reading
Purch's *Pilgrimage* at the moment of falling
asleep and his own poem was born on the

bridge between losing and gaining consciousness.

Kings and queens have been guided by dreams.

The night before he was assassinated, Caesar's wife dreamed that she saw her husband facing danger which ultimately resulted in his death.

The Fall of Troy was predicted in a dream.

It is said that Columbus heard a voice in a dream in which God promised to give him the keys of the ocean. The words came clear and bold. He held to the promise and it gave him the courage he needed so desperately in order to proceed with his plans.

Dreams of warning may also come to the bed of the dreamer.

Napoleon dreamed he was in danger. He saw himself being driven in his carriage, fleeing from the battlefield. Every detail was vivid. He saw himself crossing the river during a heavy flood—his escape lighted by torches.

But did he escape?

The dream kept recurring, warning Napoleon that he would come to a tragic end. It foretold his fate, as he was convinced that it would, for Napoleon was a firm believer in the occult and often consulted fortune tellers and seers.

What is a dream?

What produced that remarkable dream of

precognition which Mark Twain experienced—
or Napoleon's message of warning?

What causes man to dream?

Do dreams have meaning—or are they
meaningless?

Are you to heed—or brush aside—the vision
that comes to you in the dead of the night?

Are dreams your oracles—trustworthy as
they prophesy—or is it best to label those noc-
turnal visions as so much rubbish to be cleared
from your mind and carted away?

What reason can you give for the dream in
which you committed the murder that left you
so depressed upon awakening? It haunted you
all through the day, casting its gloom on your
spirit and making you heavy-hearted without
either rhyme or reason. The fact remained that
you had murdered no one. Of course, you
would have liked to strangle the boss, but your
hands were clean of blood.

Those dreams of violence—why did they
visit your bedside so often?

What made you act so violently—so unlike
your gentle self—as you choked your husband
in his sleep?

And, what a wonderful sensation of relief—
to find upon awakening—that your husband
was still alive beside you on his pillow, re-
sponding to your hugs and kisses with exclama-
tions of surprise at your unaccustomed show of
affection!

And what about that dream of yours which

had you walking naked up and down Fifth Avenue?

The odd part about the shameful act was the amazing realization that your being naked did not even embarrass you. You took walking about in your skin in your stride just like the others who appeared on the scene of your dream, accepting their nudity as a matter of course.

Thank God, you told yourself, as you bolted upright in bed, your window-shopping in the nude with visions of yourself before Tiffany's and Cartier's was just a flight of fancy. Or— and then the sly question raises its snake-like head—was there any connection between your own display and the display in the window, as if your subconscious were reminding you of your deep-rooted longing to wear a magnificent diamond—and, as so often in a dream—finally finding fulfillment?

Ever since the beginning of time, dreams have been filled with portent. They have wielded a mystic power over mankind. They have spoken in visions that led to war and beat the drum of silence that foretold both fortune and famine.

Dreams have frightened man. They have warned him. They have guided him. They have mystified him. They have terrified him. And they have comforted, healed and helped him.

Man has found the future in his dreams. He has seen the past in many a symbol. Your dream is a continuation of the present, according to the scientist, for it is then your psychic self rises to its station and operates during sleep.

Mystics regard sleep as the little sister of death, claiming that the soul leaves the body during sleep. It is then the subconscious mind, which possesses the ability to transcend time and space, takes over, going off to higher planes in order to attend schools of study, visiting entities who have passed on and assumed the spiritual form, opening windows into a vast universe which has scarcely been tapped, yet is full of potential far beyond human comprehension.

The subconscious mind never sleeps.

You live in two worlds at the same time—an outer and an inner world. You dream, whether you remember your dreams or forget them.

When you sleep, you withdraw from the world of thought all around you. You enter into your own world of thought, deep into that expanse which is sometimes referred to as the basement of the brain. This area, so full of mystery, has always fascinated man and sent him scurrying to dig for the elusive treasure that has been hidden from him in strata too deep for exploration.

Man has made—and continues to make—intensive studies and extensive experiments. Yet, in spite of his learned theories, the dream world persists in both intriguing and baffling him.

Some inroads have been made. Some of the mysteries have been revealed. Some of the clues have been called out from behind the scene with the prospect of more to come in order for you to see—and interpret—the drama of your dream.

Perhaps you are faced with a problem which seems beyond solution. You think about it all day long. No answer is in sight.

You take it to bed with you. It drops into your subconscious. You awaken in the morning. And there, to your surprise—is the perfect answer—the remedy for your ill—the person for your deal—the speech for your lecture —the sermon for next Sunday.

You ask yourself, often somewhat sheepishly, why couldn't you have thought of it? Surely, you had given it enough sweat and deliberation.

At times, it appears as if an entity—almost separate from you—is operating for you.

Who is he?

What is it?

Why is it smarter than you?

At times, much as you hesitate to concede it, you become aware of the fact that your conscious mind must be put to one side in order for your subconscious mind to get to work for you. And work it will—both willingly and hard

—provided you believe. The subconscious does not work for those who do not believe in it.

Since you spend a great portion of your life in sleep, there is a technique—a method which you can apply in order to turn your dreams into realities.

This is known as "dreaming true." It involves that you clean your conscious mind of everything you do not want to produce while giving definite directions to your subconscious to attain your desires. It is well to impress your wish upon your mind just before you fall asleep. The thought will drop like a seed into the field of your dream, developing during the night by a sort of incubation, ultimately giving expression to the full-grown desire in its rise toward the sun of your waking state.

Prime the pump by a few moments of prayer or meditation. In this way, you establish a close relationship with the higher forces to whom you can turn for help in any situation.

Make your thought intense. The intensity of your thought produces tiny magnetic lines which go out into the ether like telephone wires, carrying your message of need—and returning with the good news of achievement.

In the morning, the problem that seemed so formidable has dissolved. The task is now easier to tackle. The deal, you are now assured, will be consummated.

Dreams serve other purposes as well. Repress an emotion and the body collects a toll.

But sublimation may be reached—in a dream —and the dreamer now discovers he is free of neurosis.

Dreams aid you beyond measure to bear the wear and tear of your waking hours.

At least—in your dream—if not otherwise— you can create the life you would like to lead. If you are ill—you can dream you are well. The man who is poor can dream he is rich. The girl who is ugly can dream she is beautiful beyond words—as, in a dream, she lies in the arms of her lover.

The old adage of the grass being greener in the other fellow's pasture applies to you and your world of dreams.

Why take trips to the South Seas, Africa, Egypt and Spain? Perhaps the Grand Canyon, Niagara Falls, the Painted Desert—and all the other wonders of the world invite you to adventure.

But the most exhilarating and exciting tour you could ever make while you live on this earth is the one in which you enter upon your inner life—through the dream in your mind which is the connecting corridor between you and the Great Power that is everywhere. Here it is—waiting for you to open the door to your amazing other self!

It is here—when you seek—that you find untold treasure. It is here—when you probe— that the mystery of your dreams will be re-

vealed to you. It is here—in your dreams—
that you can transform the course of your life
and set your compass to take you to new
shores!

Chapter 2

For when dreams increase, empty words grow many; but do you fear God.
—Ecclesiastes **5:7**

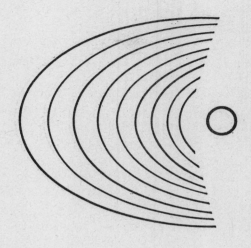

MAN HAS ALWAYS DREAMED. HE HAS ALWAYS sought to find a meaning in his dream.

The dream interpreter who made it his profession, has been plying his art for thousands of years, called both to court and to the common market place of ancient Babylon, Judea and Chaldea.

Greece exalted her diviners. The people considered dreams a channel by which contact could be made with supernatural powers. The dream diviner was held in the same high regard as the lawyer or physician of the realm and was paid a fitting fee for his services.

Both Rome and Athens boasted of their superb caliber of interpreter. The method used in that day somewhat resembles the psychoanalysis we have with us today.

An appointment would be made with the client. The interview would then proceed. It would first be preceded by a lengthy session of questions and answers. Subsequently, in a great show of fanfare, the diviner would deign to hear the dream in all its details and go about the business of reading into it the interpretation made possible by his skill.

This was sometimes at variance with the opinion of a rival diviner, who might be approached in order to procure a contradictory testimony or a more favorable fortune.

However, the interest in dreams was intense. The interpreters were kept busy, day and night, plying their trade. The philosophers of the era —many of them famous to this day—expounded at great length on the subject, certain of an audience at every turn.

Hippocrates made news by his revolutionary theory which maintained that the reason one dreamed was because, during sleep, the soul was free of the body and could wander the world at will, touching events of the past as well as those of the future.

What was the past?

What was the future?

The populace clamored for knowledge on the subject, no matter who shouted it from the market place.

However, it found cause to frown upon Cicero.

Cicero claimed that dreams were merely the result of that which happened during the dreamer's waking hours. According to Cicero, the indigestible meal of the night before was alone responsible for the dreamer's subsequent nightmare. The familiar events of the day merely entered the door of sleep as the guest of the sleeper. Why was there such a mystery in dreaming?

Yet even Cicero could not sway the public away from the magic contained in the dream and the magnet in the hands of the diviner. The public insisted on disclosing its dreams, going to great lengths to have them interpreted —no matter how far the journey to the distant oracle or the price of the fee that was exacted.

Great men of the day wrote volumes dealing with the dreamer and his dream.

Homer paid open homage to Mercury in a glowing account of the dream he had brought to Zeus.

Plato, Socrates and Aristotle were among the many celebrated authors who were renowned for their works on dreams. Here was a subject which kept the world of the day enthralled, hungry for light in the darkness of what took place during sleep.

Artemidorus, the Greek soothsayer, who lived in the long ago of 150 A.D. went to great lengths to gather up the interpretations as well as the divinations of dreams. In fact, he compiled a dream dictionary consisting of five volumes entirely devoted to dreams! He may well have been the first author to discourse on the subject.

Syria and Babylonia regarded the dream in the same light as that of religion, approaching the art of divination with reverence, sacred enough to be worshipped. Their interpreters were often elected to the post of officers of the court, and given the high rank as "Masters of the Secret Things."

Dreams were the sisters of sculpture, and considered deserving of the work of skilled artisans who recorded them upon the monuments of Egypt. Recent excavations have produced a treasure house of elaborate carvings, giving evidence of the high regard in which the dream world was held.

Public interest in the occult seemed to be at its peak at the time, particularly in Egypt and in Greece, the two nations which were far in advance of any other on the face of the earth.

They excelled in art and science. They revered the work of the goldsmith and the silversmith. They loved the beauty of the jewel and the jewel of the mind. Their priests were both

learned and highly skilled in the art of interpretation.

They maintained that sleep hid a precious
secret which only the dream could reveal, and
that the key lay locked in the locked hand of
the diviner.

It was also the custom to consult the Oracle.
In fact, the Delphic Oracle was held in such
high esteem that few men would take either a
journey or start a new venture without first
seeking the counsel at the famous altarhead
either in person or by courier.

There is a story told about King Croesus of
Lydia. He decided to test the Oracle in order
to prove its efficacy.

The test he conceived was not only prepos-
terous but far-fetched in every detail. He demanded to know just what he might be doing at
a given hour of the day. How skilled was the
diviner at divining?

King Croesus called for a brass cauldron, a
lamb, and a tortoise, officiating in person as
cook. Then he sent off a summons to the
priestess at far-off Delphi to come forth with
a report on his performance. To his amazement, his every move had been clearly seen in
spite of the distance involved. Of course, the
King was sufficiently impressed and subsequently consulted the Oracle regarding important matters relating to the kingdom.

Delphi—like many of the other Oracles of
the day, was situated high on a mountain. An

Oracle might lie hidden away, deep in a cave where silence and shadows spoke of seclusion.

Here the High Priestess made her dwelling place, dreamed her visions and revealed them to those who sought a divination. Here the High Priest received the sick and ailing who came for healing, sanctuary, help and counseling.

At times, the High Priestess or Priest would be the one to dream, diagnose the case and prescribe the medication.

At times, the patient would be the dreamer.

The process took various forms.

The patient might be required to fast, sacrifice an animal, lie down upon its skin and go to sleep. He would relate his dream upon awakening. It would then be interpreted and a cure effected of either body or affairs.

Another procedure often put into practice was somewhat more involved.

The subject would be made to bathe. The bath would be followed by the application of a sacred oil applied all over the body. A gift of sweets would be offered to the Forces the sleeper was about to meet in his sleep. He then retired to rest and to dream, awakening refreshed and ready to reveal what had appeared to him in the way of a dream during his period of sleep.

The popularity of the Oracle came to an end with the advent of Christianity during the Middle Ages.

Saints took the place of the priest and the priestess who had once presided in the high office of the diviner. Now the church became the healing center.

However, dreams were still the source often sought as a means of counseling and a way to aid the sick and the ailing.

Old records reveal the unwavering faith in which dreams were regarded even in that day and age. The story is told of Emperor Justinian who was on the point of death. He fell into a deep sleep, sinking into a coma from which it was feared he would never awaken. A vision came to him. He dreamed that the saints surrounded his bedside in an effort to save his life. The prayers they chanted over him were both loving and potent. When he woke from his sleep, he found himself fully recovered.

The news spread. The palace where his healing took place became a shrine for pilgrims.

The famous Joan of Arc, a humble peasant girl, rose to the rank of a general on a white horse, as she rode her army to victory—the victory that was first a vision and nothing more. For her great dream, she was burned at the stake, but sainthood was the monument she left behind her in a shrine that remained ever green. Bernadette was another great visionary with Lourdes as her living monument.

Now, the shrine came into favor, becoming extremely popular as a place of worship. Now change touched the hearts of mankind.

The pagan deities of old gave way to the saints of the church who took their place as healers and helpers of the helpless.

Churches were dedicated for the sole purpose of prayer and supplication. Churches raised their spires throughout the lands. The Emperor Constantine dedicated two of these churches in Byzantium. They became celebrated centers, calling mankind to their doors in search of surcease, success, healing and happiness.

Here it was—the Christian Oracle which now made its appearance.

Lourdes, the best known of them all, is attributed to a vision. Its reputation to effect cures and grant wishes is undisputed. It is believed that angels are always present, appearing to the devout in answer to prayer.

Yet, in spite of the fervor which religion brought to the scene of that day, both witchcraft and magic were still practiced. The supernatural reared its ugly head all during the Middle Ages. Devils abounded in dreams and walked abroad in daylight, busy at their evil deeds and dreaded spells which they cast upon city and village.

Religion became revolution, led by fanatics, who, in the name of God, committed the most hideous crimes.

Magicians were massacred. Witches were burned. Cats were collected in bags and baskets and thrown on pyres during certain days dedicated to saints. Superstition prevailed everywhere, often in the guise of worship.

However, dreams still held their own. Music, song and verse were used to encourage the dreamer to dream.

Measures were taken to induce visions now just as in the past when Cortez conquered Mexico. The strange effects of the fungus known as the mushroom represented medicine, food, entertainment, as well as brought on the magic of hallucination to the dreamer. This became the accepted means of travel to the heights.

Hallucinatory drugs included snuff, opium, heroin, and marijuana, among others. These were the tools of the dreamer just as they are today.

When the new age was born—a new school of scientist and philosopher arrived in its wake, able to present the new science of the action of the mind in relation to the soul during sleep.

Both Kant and Herbert Spencer wrote profusely with dreams as the subject of their text.

Freud made his appearance, posing his startling theory of dreams and their cause. He substantiated his findings by innumerable examples he collected among the patients he used in his experiments. His school of thought rose to great popularity during the early 1900's, only to eventually produce disagreement among the Freudians themselves. His work met opposition from other sources as well, including his student, Jung.

Psychologists as well as psychotherapists are now delving extensively into the dream experiences of their patients rather than dismissing them arbitrarily as so often they were prone to do in the past.

The list of scientists and researchers exploring the field of the dream is both long and illustrious. Such famous men as Hazlitt—Descartes—Havelock Ellis—Dr. Kleitman of the University of Chicago—are among the shining lights.

Even so, the dream is still eluding the greats among the scientific minds. The scientist has not as yet arrived at all the answers.

It is true that we live outside of ourselves and that sleep brings us back inside of ourselves.

But the question still plagues mankind.

What is it we find inside?

Chapter 3

In a dream, in a vision of the night, when deep sleep falleth upon men, in slumberings upon the bed; then he openeth the ears of men, and sealeth their instruction.
—Job 33:14-16

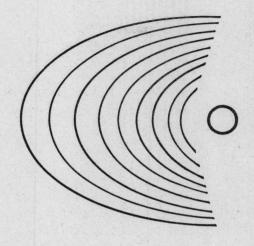

You SPEND ONE-THIRD OF YOUR LIFE IN
sleep. Some experts set this figure even higher.

They contend that if you live to the age of
a hundred, you more or less give fifty years
over to sleeping and dreaming. This figure is
not an exaggeration since your infancy is spent
in a subconscious state until you are trained in
the use of your conscious mind.

Then old age creeps upon you and your

mentality deteriorates. You begin to retreat from a life of activity and give more hours over to sleep. Now you dream more than ever, practically taking to the dream plane where you find it pleasant to meet and greet the people and the memories of the past.

Your dreams, too, change along with the years. The visions grow hazy, heavily veiled in time.

Age seems to have a profound effect upon the dream of the adult. Dreams of falling, drowning, illness, misfortune or finding a fortune dominate the sleep of the sleeper.

Children fashion their own panorama. As a rule, when they are very young, they dream of witches, tigers, and other wild animals. When they grow up, they dream of burglars, fairy tales with happy endings, Santa Claus, holidays, happy times.

Dreams are so varied, it is almost impossible to find a reason for their being, label them with purpose or classify them into exacting categories. They can stem from any number of causes and root from the seed of a memory you planted in the dim past and have long since placed in the mothballs of your conscious mind.

The visions which you see in your sleep may come about because of something you heard the day before—something you ate the night before—the condition of the mattress upon

which you are resting—the fact you are well—
or ill—or thirsty—or starved for love.

The manner in which you sleep often affects
the type of dream you experience.

Perhaps your nightmare is the result of your
uncomfortable position in bed. Your blankets
may have slipped from your body or are
strangling you at the moment.

Your dream may have its origin in the un-
likeliest setting of some foreign country you
never saw in your life. You may catch yourself kissing either the ugliest or the most handsome man in the world.

Perhaps you have fallen asleep flat on your
back. You begin to feel seasick. You dream
you are at sea in a boat that is sinking.

Perhaps a loose shutter is banging outside
your window in the wind. Your dream may
take the shape of your facing a firing squad at
daybreak with the sound of the bullets thundering all around you.

What causes such dreams?

How can you explain them?

Where do you go during sleep?

Sleep—producing the dream state—continues to baffle science. We know that during
the waking state, the conscious ego acts directly
upon the conscious or wide-awake mind, and
that during sleep, the ego acts entirely upon
the subconscious. As you fall asleep, all the
thoughts, desires, intentions, tendencies, feelings and ideas that have accumulated during

the day sink down into that subconscious, creating a maze of mystifying dreams.

Sleep acts like a hopper into which all sorts of emotions and sensations are poured. You can scarcely name all the other ingredients which mix and mingle, boil and bubble, cook for hours or even years down in those bottomless depths of your being.

This concoction is known as sleep. It serves innumerable purposes.

Sleep reveals.

Sleep refreshes.

Sleep directs and guides.

Sleep is a warning sign-post.

Sleep is a comforter.

Sleep is all things to all people.

Yet what is sleep?

Why do we sleep?

The medical profession maintains that sleep —true sleep—is often a delusion. You never really sleep. Your brain is wide awake and active even in sleep.

Your brain centers which govern your sight, your hearing and your smell never sleep. Sleep does not take over the optic, auditory, olfactory and gustatory nerves.

The subconscious continues to carry on while you sleep. Your heart keeps right on beating. Your lungs keep right on breathing. Your blood continues to circulate.

This has been attested by the fact that people have been known to walk in their sleep.

Soldiers on march, weighted down by heavy loads, have been seen to sleep-walk, arriving rested and alert at their destination.

Such celebrated scientists as Hazlitt and Descartes belonging to the early school which dealt with the mind, contended that mankind dreamed all night, remembering only fragments of that which took place. They declared that the mind was always alert even when in sleep. The mind never slept. It had a reason for dreaming.

Subsequently, scientists of note have made various attempts to study the reasons and dissect them as if performing an autopsy.

While no decisive conclusions have been reached, it is conceded in some quarters—while argued down in others—that your dream is the result of the life that you lead.

Your dream may deal with some physical problem due to the state of your health. It is via your dream that you react to improper diet, lack of exercise or some other human frailty. Your dream is the means by which your subconscious mind registers a justifiable protest.

On the other hand, your dream may be one of self-analysis which comes about because of an inner challenge you are encouraged to face and conquer.

An interesting case history is that of a woman who dreamed she was sitting before her mirror. She met an ugly sight. Wrinkles—

straggly hair and a double chin peered out at her from the glass. She dreamed she was a witch. She awoke with the determination to improve her looks—and set about to see a new face the next time she consulted her looking glass.

Perhaps, in your sleep, you meet with a psychic experience.

Psychic perception came to a mother who was awakened from deep slumber. She saw her son in danger on the battlefield and called out to warn him. Her voice, sounding so loud and so terrified in the dead of night, could not help but awaken her. She remained awake to pray for her boy.

Was it a dream, she asked herself in the morning? Was it nothing more than a dream?

It proved quite the contrary, for when her boy returned home on leave, he related what happened that very night, on that very hour. He remembered it clearly. He had heard his mother's warning. The urge came over him to order his troops to halt. In the morning, he discovered the reason for her call—and the action he had followed. The enemy had peppered the field with mines. Death would have wiped them out had they proceeded.

Death—in one form or another—often comes to stand beside your bed.

Strange as it seems, you and your bedfellow may share the same dream.

There have been instances in which husband

and wife, or even two people a great distance apart have dreamed the same dream at the same time. Perhaps the dream involved a third person. Superstition regards the appearance of the third person—when seen in a dream—as a warning of his approaching death.

Perhaps you have dreamed of someone who was very close to you in life and has passed on, leaving behind him an unsolved family problem.

The story is told of a Connecticut lawyer who had four daughters. When he died, he left a will, properly signed and witnessed, bequeathing all his money to the youngest girl. The others thought this not only very unlikely but highly unjust. However, there was nothing they could do about it. They could take no legal steps to establish an equitable division of the property.

The oldest girl, in particular, was troubled about the situation, not so much for herself and her own loss but that of her other two sisters. The matter preyed on her mind.

One night, she had a dream. She saw her father come toward her down the street upon which she lived. She went to meet him. He smiled in greeting.

He had not changed. He was dressed as always in his neat blue business suit. He cleared his throat with a little chuckle, just as she remembered he had done so often in the past, and then he proceeded to speak to her.

He told her he had made a subsequent will and that she would find it in the pocket of his bathrobe, which hung in the upstairs closet of the little house at the lake which they used as their summer camp.

At first, she decided to ignore the dream. After all, it was only a dream. But the dream repeated itself three nights in a row. It was insistence—on the part of her subconscious mind —that finally induced her to take a trip to the lake.

Sure enough, the bathrobe still hung among the rest of his clothes in the little house. And there was the last—and final will—stitched into place under the lining—just as he had described it to her in the dream. Here were his final wishes.

The will was opened. He had divided his estate equally between all four daughters.

Of course, it was declared legal. All agreed that justice had been done.

Now what reasonable explanation could be given for the series of events which had taken place?

Why had the solution come about during the sleeping rather than the waking hours?

What had brought on the dream, forcing the return of a departed spirit to right a wrong?

Was it the father?

Was it the girl?

She was honest enough to admit she had prayed often and ardently for justice to come on the scene. There is little doubt that her intensity of purpose eventually drew her father to her side.

Scientists maintain that the condition of sleep seems to be especially suitable for the reception of telepathic communications. When you enter into sleep, you invite communication with your deeper self which is known as your superconscious—or make a contact with a friend, relative or some loved one who has passed on—just as the girl had attracted and established that line of contact with her father.

It is an acknowledged fact that the subconscious accepts the impression in the form of a command and produces the corresponding expression. When you direct your subconscious in this way, the results are sure to be fruitful.

If you prepare yourself properly to sleep, you will wake up feeling refreshed. If you go to sleep with all sorts of worries and turmoils in your mind, you will wake up feeling dull and depressed. If you need guidance, you will get it.

Spiritual guidance, in numerous guises, is a familiar experience to those who believe in its efficacy—and act upon it.

Spiritual guidance came to a physician who suffered from a bad siege of bronchitis. Finally he prescribed a form of treatment for himself.

Each night, before dropping off to sleep, he prayed for healing. He talked to the cells, nerves and tissues of his lungs, suggesting that they make themselves perfect and whole in every fibre of their being.

But healing seemed to evade him. Then, one night, in a dream, he saw himself transported to the desert in Arizona. Here a healing took place in record time. Here was proof that prayer was able to release the kinetic energy of the subconscious mind, outlining the proper action for the dreamer to follow.

It is a good plan just before falling asleep to talk to your subconscious as if it were your counsellor. Outline your program for the day ahead.

Never go to sleep when you are disturbed or discouraged. This emotion will settle into the innermost part of your being and you will find yourself losing ground in your life.

Always go to sleep thinking thoughts of wealth, power and success.

Feed thoughts of health to your subconscious and it will permeate health to every part of your body.

Feed thoughts of success to your work.

Go to sleep with strong, clear ideas of harmony, power, advancement and prosperity held clearly in mind. The cause will be formed in the subconscious and its effects will appear in your life.

Your health will begin to improve.

More power will flow through your body.

Your talents will be fired with renewed inspiration.

All mankind knows the importance of sleeping on a difficult problem. An old proverb states that sleep brings wisdom.

Have you an important decision to make?

Sleep on it!

Harness your sleeping self each night by asking it to serve you—and it will!

Be sure you remember to thank it first—for giving, you will learn to your advantage, must precede, getting!

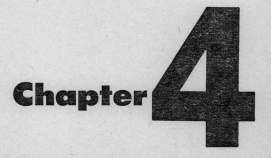

Chapter 4

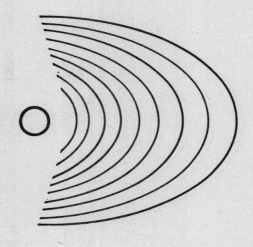

They are like a dream when one awakes, on awaking you despise their phantoms.

—Psalms 73:20

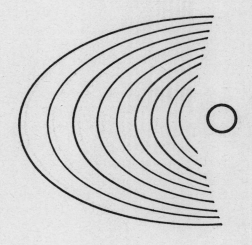

ABRAHAM LINCOLN BELIEVED IN DREAMS. A
dream prophesied his own assassination.

A few days preceding the tragedy, he told
a few friends of the disturbing vision he had
experienced after working very late one night.
In the dream, he rose from his bed, walked
down into the main hall and wandered idly
here and there through the empty rooms. He

could hear the sound of weeping. But no one was visible until he came to the East Room.

There, on a catafalque, lay a body, guarded by soldiers. A long line of people was passing by the corpse. It lay with its face covered from view.

Lincoln approached a guard. He asked who had died.

"The President—by an assassin," was the solemn reply.

Lincoln turned aside. He left the room, followed by the haunting murmur of the crowd. He went back to bed. The dream faded and he slept.

But it came to pass. He met assassination at Ford's Theatre, felled by John Wilkes Booth.

His body was laid in state in the East Room of the White House—just as he had seen it in his dream. Soldiers guarded the bier. There was the sound of quiet weeping in the halls. All was perfect as Lincoln had envisioned it, exact in every detail, just as he had told it to an audience—which assured him it was only a fancy— a hallucination due to overwork.

It is conceded that Lincoln was a spiritualist. Seances were often held at the White House. In fact, in spite of pressure from powerful groups to delay the proclamation, he proceeded with the emancipation of the slaves. The measure came about through the trance mediumship of Nettie Colburn, whom he often consulted all through his career.

Nettie Colburn would sink into a deep sleep during which her messages would emerge as if imparted to her by another entity, long gone from the earth. According to Lincoln, his spirit guide was none other than Daniel Webster whose portrait hung in a prominent place on the wall of the President's room.

And who could deny the potency of Mrs. Colburn's predictions which came into being through sleep? She not only predicted the end of the war but Lincoln's re-election. This, too, came to pass.

The President, in spite of public opinion, made no secret of the debt he owed to the woman who used the means of sleep in order to guide and inspire him. He confided to those who were close to him that he had witnessed many a marvel in the seance room, wonderful things, most of them much too secret and still to be told. They have remained untold to this day. He considered his contact with Webster a very personal one, too precious to air to an unbelieving public.

While numerous scientists place little credence in spiritualism or emphatically deny that communication between the dead and the living even exists, all sorts of strange messages travel back and forth with undisputed testimony which bears out the truth that a form of power is there, operating with little or no explanation for its existence.

Psychologists maintain that the brain is di-

vided into two distinct sections, comprising the
conscious and the subconscious.

The conscious mind works during the day. It
comes to decisions and attempts to solve problems which may trouble your waking hours. It
is apt to forget many details which affect the
situation in which you are involved.

But the subconscious remembers everything.
It forgets nothing.

In fact, filed away deep in the bottomless
interior of your being is every experience you
ever met in your life—every fact and even
every fancy.

Artists—authors—composers and other creative minds—are proof of a power which func-
tions in a most mysterious manner that even
the experts find difficult to explain. Dreaming
is the tool the artist uses.

The basic idea for the celebrated story of
Dr. Jekyll and Mr. Hyde came to Robert Louis
Stevenson in a dream that was so exact in de-
tail, he had merely to act as reporter.

According to Stevenson, dreams were plays
performed in the theatre of the mind which
was lighted long after the lights in the house
were out. The lights in the mind remained
bright all through the night. Then, while the
body was deep in slumber, the plays would begin in which the sleeper was the actor as well
as the audience of one.

Stevenson maintained that his daytimes
were unfruitful. But, at night—in that lighted

theatre of his mind—he would witness the parade of the little people as he called them, the "brownies," whom he welcomed and blessed. He acknowledged that they came to regale him with story upon story in a never-ending stream of fascinating and profitable plots.

Dr. Jekyll and Mr. Hyde were not the only epic figures which came to Stevenson in dreams. The pressure of sheer existence often acted like a priming pump. It never failed to produce the flow of a steady stream of stories.

There were periods in his life when the butcher, the baker and the banker dunned him for his debts. It was then he set his mind to work in search of plot and counterplot. It was then his dreams proved more fruitful than ever.

Goethe, who wrote Faust, confessed that his best writing hours were those when he was in a state of somnambulism. He often composed his poetry from beginning to end without even being aware he was putting words on the paper. At times, he was awakened by the scratching of his pen. In fact, while in the sleeping state, Goethe not only did his best work, but often read the future in vision which ultimately came to pass.

He foretold the Messina Earthquake. He saw himself riding a horse he did not even own at the moment.

The dream became a reality many years

later, proving to Goethe that precognition fore-
shadowed events on the screen of time.

Surely Goethe spoke in wisdom when he
said that man walked in mystery, not knowing
what is stirring in the atmosphere that sur-
rounds him, nor how it concerns his spirit. So
much is certain, declared Goethe, that man
could put out the feelers of his soul beyond
its bodily limits.

What are those limits?

Where is the boundary line?

The dream has no horizon.

Great minds—all through time—have traveled on the wings of their visions. They do not
hesitate to acknowledge their indebtedness to
their dreams. They obey the directions they
take, the vagaries involved, the methods, often
odd and unpredictable, which have to be employed.

Alfred Tennyson, the English poet, declared
that in order to work, he would first need to
induce a state of mystical ecstasy akin to sleep.
It was then he produced some of his greatest
masterpieces.

Schiller acknowledged his debt to the hours
he spent in sleep, declaring that when his human reasoning withdrew its watch at the door
of his mind, ideas came pell-mell over the
threshhold.

Robert Browning—George Sand—Charles
Dickens—Mark Twain—Victor Hugo—Jane
Austen—the list is long and impressive of

authors who used their hours of sleep in order to receive ideas and inspiration.

In my own life, many of my books have been born as a result of either a dream or a vision. My little dog, Hobo, about whom I had written so many stories and three dog books, came to me at a time of desperation in my life. The wire-haired appeared in a vision, urging me to seek the solace of work. He gave me the plot and even the title of the book, *All Dogs Go to Heaven,* which subsequently became a best seller.

Another book—a novel this time—was a command performance by a vision produced through the skill of my subconscious mind, which furnished plot, characters, color, dialogue and even took me on a series of astral travels to an air base in space—at that time not even in existence, which came to be known as *Universal Station,* the title and theme of my book.

According to Freud, when a writer dreams a story, it is his way of fulfilling some deep desire or wish. It is then he is his own hero, his character exactly opposite to what he is in life. If the writer is good, kind and thoughtful, he will dream of himself as being evil, hard and thoughtless. In this manner—an author—influenced by the unconscious—finds relief in dreams.

Some authors even go to extremes in order to secure their story material. They eat indi-

gestible food upon retiring to encourage night-
mares. According to them, a late supper which
does not agree with the stomach, makes excel-
lent fodder for science fiction.

Authors of horror and mystery stories have
confessed to gorging themselves at night, particularly when the inkwell of inspiration is dry,
awakening with a fine stock of murder and
mayhem.

Dryden ate huge quantities of raw meat in
order to envision scenes of luxury and create
characters of affluence. He welcomed the
nightly nightmare.

Drugs influence dreams. So does alcohol.

As a rule, these bring on dreams which de-
pict rats, reptiles and vermin. Hashish, Indian
hemp, marijuana, heroin, as well as the fumes
of carbon-bisulphide induce visions in which
the dreamer finds himself leaping over cliffs,
being hunted, hung or murdered—a welcome
feast for the fiction writer.

Precognition is another arrow which the
writer likes to shoot from his bow.

Many years before the airplane was invented
in 1903, Tennyson penned the most amazing
poem packed with precognition. He dipped into
the future. He saw the heavens filled with the
commerce staffed by pilots. He saw the war
waged in the skies. He saw the Parliament of
Man and the ultimate Federation of the World.

Where did *Twenty Thousand Leagues Under*

The Sea by Jules Verne come from—except from a dream which bore fruit in the future?

It is not only the good fortune of artists and authors to find ready harvests in their dreams.

Scientists, inventors, doctors, lawyers and intrepid fliers are often visited by apparitions, guided by illuminations and hunches which appear to them in their dreams.

Henry Ward Beecher, the preacher, whose daughter, Harriet Beecher Stowe, wrote *Uncle Tom's Cabin*, entirely inspired by a dream, was himself a dreamer. He was able to deliver a sermon every day for eighteen months by following a unique method. He would drop an idea into his mind, much like wheat into a mill, allowing it to incubate during the night. And, behold! There was the sermon—each and every morning, ready for its presentation on the platform.

Archbishop Temple of Canterbury conceded that all his decisive thinking took place behind the scenes during sleep.

The secret of the benzene molecule came to Kekulé while he was asleep.

The Nobel prizewinner, Otto Loewi, while fast asleep, came upon the discovery that active chemicals are involved in the action of nerves.

Businessmen, upon retiring, use the technique of getting themselves out of the way and posing their problems to the subconscious, keeping a notebook by the bedside in order to jot down any creative ideas which may be re-called immediately upon awakening.

Doctors have fallen asleep in the midst of technical research and dreamed the perfect answers.

Students have fallen asleep over their books, exhausted by their preparations for a forthcom-ing examination—only to meet the problem they envisioned in their dreams—along with its solution as if the subconscious mind of the stu-dent had peered over the shoulder of the exam-iner with the dishonest intent to cheat!

An outstanding example of the power that is present in sleep, is that of Charles Lind-bergh during his flight in *The Spirit of St. Louis*.

It seemed he had been without sleep for a day and a night preceding his advent in the air. Sleep overtook him just as he went into action. He felt a force rise up within him as well as the presence of what appeared to be ghosts riding along at his side.

They spoke to him. He recognized familiar voices from the long ago of his life. He recog-nized familiar faces of loved ones who had departed.

All through his flight, he lived in their com-pany, drawn to the past—yet remaining in the present—confident that he would reach his goal with the help of his helpers from the other side.

It is said that he was finally awakened from

sleep by the presence of a fly on his nose. The fly had made its appearance, seemingly from nowhere. It vanished in the same mysterious fashion.

The fact remains that creative activity depends in some degree on signals from the subconscious mind during sleep. It is the subconscious mind which sets to work while the conscious mind is off-duty.

You may be reading—walking—driving—enjoying your dinner or fast asleep in your bed. It is then that the conscious mind is at rest and the subconscious chooses to work, classifying facts and fancies from the buried store of your daily experiences.

What do you know?

What do you need to know?

What should you do?

Whom should you see?

How do you go about the project close at hand?

Is there an answer to any of the many problems you are forever facing as you walk through life?

Yes!

Go to sleep!

Dream!

Pass your need along to that hard-working, willing servant of yours—your subconscious mind!

Yes.

Your subconscious—while you are asleep—

can dream great dreams for you. It can compose great symphonies which have eluded your waking senses. It can open closed doors to every avenue of your being, revealing secrets to inventions, warnings for your safety, guidance for your good.

Call on it to work for you—and it will lift up your ambitions and set them down before you as realities!

Chapter 5

"In a dream, in a vision of the night, when deep sleep falls upon men, while they slumber on their beds, then he opens the ears of men, and terrifies them with warnings, that he may turn man aside from his deed, and cut off pride from man; he keeps back his soul from the Pit, his life from perishing by the sword."

—Job 33:15

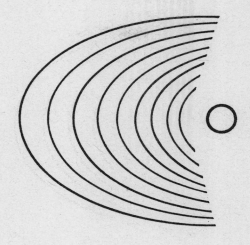

DREAMS OFTEN SERVE AS BAROMETERS.

They reveal the state of your health as well as that of your bank account. They are mirrors of your joys as well as that of your sorrows. You carry your worries to bed with you when you go to sleep and they lie on the pillow beside you to take shape in dreams that leave you shaken and depressed.

Dreams may be motivated by physical, mental and emotional reactions to the external experiences you meet throughout your day. These engage the lower levels of your mind.

There are also dreams in which you enter a deep state of consciousness which enables you to make contact with a friend or a loved one. Under these conditions, information which you may have been seeking is imparted to you as if an entity apart from you had appeared from afar to do your bidding or aid you in solving a problem. The solution which may be dramatized in a dream sequence is so vivid that you cannot help but recall it upon awakening in details so exact they resemble reality.

It is also possible that you contact an entity —in the person of someone you have loved and lost—or an entity makes an effort to establish a contact with you and communicate something of importance to you while you are sleeping. It may be something that troubles you or a mystery which has never been solved.

The story is told of a beautiful young bride who was drowned in a lake while on her honeymoon.

The Coast Guard was summoned. Grapplers searched the waters thoroughly from shore to shore. In spite of all efforts, her body could not be found. There was nothing to do but to leave the site of the tragedy.

However, the young husband refused to abandon the search. He remained long after the summer was over and the last of the seasonal boarders had deserted the place.

One night, he fell into an uneasy sleep. His wife appeared to him in his dream. She led him to a cove filled with rotting tree stumps and pointed to a mass of brush. Then she smiled assurance and the vision faded.

Sure enough, the dream pointed to the subsequent discovery. Her body was found in the cove under the mass of brush where the waves of a violent summer storm had wedged it in place.

The divers thought to humor the husband when they combed the spot he indicated. But there it was—the proof that a soul could return and deliver a meaning message.

Your dream can take the form of a piece of important information which is necessary to your business. By harnessing your dream to fulfillment, that subconscious mind of yours will emerge with the plan, idea, inspiration and insight that proves best for you to follow. Your dream can give you direction—which is not apparent to your waking senses—as in the case of the young bridegroom.

It has the amazing ability to sense or foresee an event that is to take place in the future. This form of dream, which involves extrasensory perception has baffled experts since time began. Here is a dream state that cannot be explained.

Here is a force which breaks through your

subconscious into the area of your conscious awareness, often carrying with it such a sense of conviction that it merits nothing less than the most serious consideration on your part.

Do not stifle or discourage the functioning of this precognitive faculty. Be alert at all times to recognize any manifestation which may appear to either guide or warn you. There is always sure to be a reason for the warning.

The experience of a young nurse is a case in point.

One night, while at home, she dreamed she was still on duty at the hospital. She was walking through the ward—in her dream—when she saw an overhead lighting fixture swinging perilously, back and forth, threatening to fall on her patient and crush him to death.

The terrifying dream awoke her. She did not wait until morning, but dressed, hailed a cab and raced to the hospital.

The attendants were surprised to see her during her off-duty hours. They shook their heads knowingly as she told them of her dream. One of them whispered something or other about her being crazy when she insisted on moving the patient and all his paraphernalia.

They were in the process of bringing a ladder to place under the fixture in order to examine it, when, to their amazement, it fell to the floor of its own volition, crashing down in a thundering shower of iron and glass.

The laughter ceased as suddenly as it had

started when she first related her dream. Here was the sober realization that the dream had saved a life!

Scientists claim that you dream every night whether you can recall your dream or are not able to recall a single detail.

That subconscious mind of yours which never sleeps is endowed with an intelligence which is beyond all human comprehension. It is there, standing guard, day and night over your sleeping state.

Otherwise, how can you explain the tremendous power inherent in the consciousness to forestall even the advent of death when it appears to be inevitable, striking someone you love?

Who is it needs your help?

The story is told of a mother whose son was stationed in the South Pacific. One night, she dreamed that a tremendous tropical tree, lashed by a gale, was about to fall on the tent where he slept along with his companions, threatening to kill all the occupants.

She awoke, bathed with sweat, shook her husband out of his sleep and related her dream. Together, they knelt in prayer, calling on God to protect the sleeping men.

Sure enough, several weeks later, a letter arrived from their son. He wrote he had gone to bed at an early hour. A tropical storm struck the area.

At first, he merely dreamed that he heard

two people praying. He recognized the familiar voices of his mother and his father, took it as a sign of warning, ordered the men from their cots. They grumbled at the prospect of going out into the storm. But when the giant tree struck the tent and flattened it to earth, along with their beds and their belongings, they knew that their lives had been saved.

What is it troubles you?

Who is it troubles you?

Why?

What should you do?

Where can you go?

Whom can you call?

Give the problem over to your subconscious mind.

Sleep on it!

Yes.

Sleep on it!

Suppose you find yourself in a quandary regarding your affairs. You are drawn deep into sleep.

You transmit the thought to your subconscious mind. It absorbs your problem. It acts upon it.

It is then your task—the task of the receiver, to pull back the subconscious thought into the field of conscious awareness, so that, upon awakening, you have the picture—the message —the solution—or whatever else you require to meet your need.

The way to do this is to consciously feed

your mind—a few minutes before you fall asleep—with definite order of what you want that subconscious mind of yours to do—how it is to function—what it is you want produced.

Do not try to get behind the mysterious workings of how this is achieved. Remember the adage, so full of wisdom, which said that it was curiosity which killed the cat!

When William Lear, who is the head of the Lear Electronics Company, predicted that a day would come when you would be able to reduce your body to a stream of electrons—beam them out into space and assemble them at that point, the experts scoffed. But science has since proven that mass can be converted into energy and back into mass again.

In the same manner, who is to say that the physical body of the individual is the real self? The real self is more apt to be the spiritual entity. Actually, it is your spirit and not your physical being, which is the home of your consciousness.

And here, is this home, you can produce wonders and miracles beyond all imagination!

Chapter 6

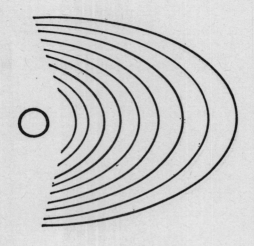

Thou shalt be secure, because there is hope: yea, . . . thou shalt take thy rest in safety.

—Job 11:18-19

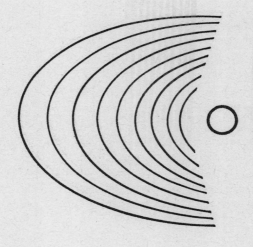

NAPOLEON WAS A DEVOUT BELIEVER IN THE occult.

His mother had foretold his fortune. She was certain of his future. Just before he was born, she related, she had a vivid dream that she would give birth to an eagle, an indisputable sign that her infant would grow up to hold a high rank in the world and become famous in time to come. She saw a vision of the humble peasant boy who had no social status at the moment in the exalted position as a leader of men.

Napoleon believed her. He believed without a doubt that his star would rise in the sky and remain there to shine forever. He paid frequent visits to fortune-tellers and diviners, all of whom prophesied his success and great fortune.

Although his mother was certain that Napoleon would win the race, since the eagle was regarded as the swiftest bird on the wing, the diviners of the present day differ with her interpretation.

As a matter of fact, it is known that the eagle drives away other birds, and, in the process of their flying off in order to escape, is apt to be left behind. Perhaps this reading is closer to the truth since it spells out Napoleon's ultimate fate!

Birds, it seems, have always intrigued the practicing psychic.

The dream of a bird does not indicate freedom and song. Instead, it is claimed that a bird symbolizes the approach of death. The vision of a dove—in a dream—sets the time at exactly three days before the spirit of the sleeper leaves his own body.

Everyone dreams.

Every dream you dream, no matter how ridiculous, far-fetched or ephemeral, has a meaning behind it.

True, a dream may appear to be nothing

more than a fantasy. Yet, upon review, it can be seen to have some sort of logic, be presented in some sort of order, and if nothing else, serve a purpose in the mental well-being of the person.

Perhaps a husband is nagged by his wife. He accepts her daily abuses meekly. But at night, in his sleep, he is the one in command. He is the captain at the wheel of the ship, the master with the whip beating his female slave unmercifully.

The dream—in this case—may remain nothing more than a dream and the husband may continue to live a life of abject misery. On the other hand, it may stir him to action. It may make him stand up and assert himself, much to his wife's amazement. A reformation may even result!

Perhaps you are holding down a job that you hate. Your boss is demanding, critical, unfair, and unappreciative. Each day that you come to work under his relentless eye, spells another day of torture for you.

But you cannot afford to resign. The money is good and your family requires your earnings.

Yes, it may be that your working hours are hours of torture. But at night, in your sleep, your position at the office is reversed. You are in the place of power. You no longer cringe to your employer. You face him boldly and with confidence.

Well, you tell yourself upon awakening, it

was only a dream. Why only a dream, you ask?
Why not make it a reality? Why not stand up
to the boss and look him squarely in the eye?
Why not face the jeers of the office force with
good humor and in good grace?

It worked—in a dream!

And so, the dream takes over, with wonderful results—the springboard found in sleep. It
begins to act in daily life as the rewarded experience. To your surprise, your boss com-
mences to change his attitude toward you.
Since you no longer cringe to him, he now
respects you. The other employees also join
the ranks of admirers who say good morning
with a smile—and actually mean it!

Negative dreams can be turned into positive
ones, enriching every day of your life. Look
for the guidance they point out to you.

At times, a dream will repeat itself not only
once but twice and possibly even three times,
as if to impress the sleeper to take steps in a
given direction.

At times, even the steps are outlined. Many
a murder has been solved in this fashion.

Mediums, in trance, have come upon muti-
lated bodies which have been buried away. In
fact, under trance, one medium actually saw
the murder re-enacted in the living room where
it had taken place.

She claimed that the vibrations which were
left behind in the form of a residue created a
picture which still hung in the ether, almost

like a painting, somewhat misty yet clear enough to distinguish the various figures.

Far-fetched as it seems, experiments with a sensitive camera have been conducted by both experts and novices, and photographs taken of rooms in which crimes have been committed. The clues must be recent for an imprint to appear on the negative since the people involved are prone to fade from the scene.

In the case of this particular medium, she not only envisioned the murder but she saw the murderer bury the corpse under a tree.

The police were called in. The body was located in the burial place she had designated. The murderer confessed to the crime and was subsequently imprisoned.

Another murder, solved in a dream, concerned a young farm wife who disappeared from home under mysterious circumstances.

Since she lived in the middle West, her parents, who lived in the East, were not aware of her death. Her husband kept writing cheerful letters to them, assuring them that she was well and happy. She was busy, he wrote, too busy and too lazy to sit down and send off a letter.

The father accepted the flimsy excuse. The mother, however, was somewhat doubtful. Her woman's intuition kept nudging at her day and night.

One night she had a dream. She saw her daughter in a vision, her arms outstretched in pleading, her eyes brimming over with tears. The vision faded.

But this time, the mother took the heeding to heart. She induced her husband to make the trip West. They went unannounced to the farm. The vision had revealed where the body had been buried. It lay under the floor of the barn.

It was here they found the remains wrapped in a blanket. Identification was established by the dental work since all else was in a state of decay. Their daughter had been dead for several years, a clear case of murder, for which the farmer was indicted.

It is the firm belief of metaphysicians, that, when one looks to God for guidance to solve a mystery or right a wrong, the answer may come by reaching out to man by means of dreams. They claim that intuitive feelings are not the only avenue for receiving direction.

According to them, it is not enough to gather up the snatches here and there and attempt to weave the finished tapestry.

You must look to the beginning of your dream for the initial cause that is responsible for your problem. You must go to the end to find the solution.

This procedure was borne out in the true account of Madame Harteville, the widow of the Dutch Ambassador in Stockholm.

It seemed that before he died, he had bought her an expensive gift of silver. To her surprise, the silversmith appeared soon after, demanding payment.

Madame Harteville was stunned by the demand. She knew her husband well enough to know he was too honest to have left an unsettled debt behind him.

The days passed. The bill collector's visits increased to the point of harassment.

Finally, in desperation, she sought out Swedenborg, the renowned mystic. Could he communicate with her husband, she inquired, to ascertain the true state of affairs?

Swedenborg consented to help her.

Three days later, he called to report that he had contacted her husband. The bill for the silver service had been paid and receipted. She would find the papers in a drawer of the bureau upstairs in the bedroom.

Madame Harteville searched each and every drawer of the bureau. Her search proved fruitless.

She returned to Swedenborg, intent upon reproving him for the false report. There were no papers in the bureau. Every drawer was empty.

Swedenborg retorted she was wrong. He informed her that the bureau contained a secret compartment she had failed to open. The receipt for the silver was inside. He would accompany her back to her home in order to prove he was right.

They went upstairs to the bedroom. There was the bureau. Swedenborg found the secret drawer. Inside were the proper papers, establishing that the silver service had been paid for seven months prior to the Ambassador's death.

Another account of alleged nonpayment involves a young Broadway actor who was being sued for a debt he had paid several years before. He had been on the road with a stock company for so long a run that the receipt for the money was lost. His case, too, would be lost, his lawyer told him, unless he produced either the papers or a witness to the fact that he had made the payment.

Night after night, he went to bed torn by the prospect of meeting the sum which threatened to wipe out his earnings for a year. A jail sentence stared him in the face. He did not know where to turn or whom to call on for help.

One night, in a dream, he saw his father who had died a year ago. His father spoke to him. He gave him the name of the witness who had been present when the money exchanged hands.

The actor sought out the witness who was only too willing to appear in his behalf.

The lawyer took his deposition. The situation was saved.

Dreams are replete with warnings.

A housewife dreamed that her house had been looted. Money—jewelry—and other valuables had been removed from the premises during the night.

When she awoke the next morning, over

their eight o'clock coffee, she related her dream to her husband.

Of course, he laughed at her story. But when he searched the house, he found it was so. The kitchen door had been forced open. They had been robbed during the night.

Dreams deliver warnings which often come to pass.

At times, dreams involving plane wrecks induce a passenger to cancel a flight without any reason for doing so, only to be met by the report which follows soon after to verify the catastrophe.

Dr. Walter Prince, the celebrated psychical researcher, once had a dream that he saw a train crash in a tunnel. Every detail was clear as a picture. The smoke, the steam, the cries of the passengers, and the figures of the rescuers appeared before him. He awoke his wife to recount the dream. Sure enough, news came of a train wreck in a tunnel with the drama repeated exactly as Dr. Prince had envisioned it.

You may dream of a friend or relative about to be hospitalized. You see the hospital room in all its detail. The news comes of your friend's illness, corroborating the dream. You visit the room. It is familiar to you. You saw it in your dream.

Always pay attention to your dream. It is trying to tell you something you need to know. There may be something you need to do.

Record it immediately when you awaken,

no matter how strange, how impossible, fantastic and unbelievable your dream may have been.

Always view your dream in a serious light, not as something emerging idly during a night of sleep.

Dreams have come to be regarded as extremely important by the psychologist, aiding him in interpreting unconscious mental processes.

They give the physician a clearer understanding of such abnormal mental states as phobias, obsessions, delusions, and hallucinations.

They are considered a potent instrument for the removal of the symptoms arising out of functional nervous disturbances.

The dream is the real interpreter of human life—and can radically change the pattern of your life!

It is the guideline for the believer, the healer for the ill, the friend for the friendless.

Cherish your dream—and it will serve you when you have a problem to solve!

Chapter 7

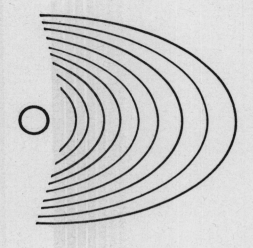

*Ye shall lie down, and none shall
make you afraid.*

—Leviticus 26:6

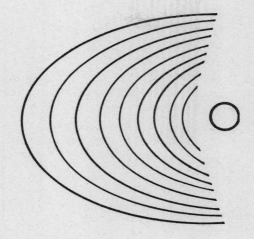

Anything can happen——in a dream.

If you are weak, you may see yourself as being strong and virile, vibrant with good health.

If you are afraid of water, you see yourself in the role of an Olympic champion, surrounded by autograph hunters. You may even dream the impossible. You use your many medals as water wings and they save you and your beautiful companion from drowning!

If you have no one who loves you, you see yourself in the midst of a passionate love affair. You even dream every detail of the drama.

You walk into a room dressed in the elegant clothes of a princess. A handsome prince enters, bearing the gift of a ring which he slips on your finger, murmuring words of love. But, just as you are about to meet his lips with your own, the alarm clock goes off. You are rudely awakened to the fact that if you do not get up in a hurry, dress and go to work, you will miss your train and be fired from your job.

Why, you ask yourself, did you dream of grandeur and wake up to the grim reality of your humdrum days?

Freud would be inclined to stress the objective interpretation, involving that of sex, which, no doubt, is what you now lack in your life.

Jung would accent the subjective, embodying your wish fulfillment. According to Jung, your desire for Prince Charming produces the gallant suitor.

It is true that, at times, your dreams of sex may shock you. There is no reason for you to be embarrassed.

Do not condemn yourself. Your subconscious mind is simply achieving in the dream state the things you refuse to do while in your waking state.

It is perfectly normal for you to lose your

conscious personality. You are now acting at a level below the threshold of consciousness. Various ideas, desires, fears, memories, warnings and apparitions create new and often absurd relationships, concocting fantastic adventures which you see in the form of visions.

But the interesting feature about sleep is the fact that since your voluntary being is temporarily suspended, you are behaving openly and honestly! You have nothing to hide. At last you can be yourself!

A lover pursues you. You love it!

You stole a gold watch you admired at the jeweler's. You keep it!

You make a play for a neighbor's husband. You sail in his sailboat with him, his arms entwined around your waist.

You buy a car. You hire a chauffeur!

You refuse to pay your rent. Your landlord is down on his knees to *you!*

You ask your boss for a raise. You get it!

Dreaming, you decide, is wonderful, for nothing is denied to you. No one is inaccessible —not even that neighbor's husband.

However, you must try to remember that all these bright baubles will break when you wake —for they are only the means your subconscious mind is taking to try and please you.

Yet your subconscious mind may suddenly decide to reverse itself and play a serious role in your life. It is then that you can depend on the signals it sends you while you are asleep.

The story is told of a couple who were about to go out to dinner. The husband who had placed his watch in the bureau, was concerned by the fact it was missing. Both husband and wife searched the room thoroughly without finding the watch.

That night—the wife, in a dream, saw the husband putting the watch into the pocket of the suit he had discarded in the process of changing into his evening clothes. Sure enough, the next morning, there it was—just as it had been depicted in her dream.

Harness your sleeping self each night by asking it to serve you—and it will!

Accept the truism that in reality, you are actually one person having two distinct lives, as well as two sets of senses. Each day, you use your body as your physical being, judging and reasoning entirely from the basis of your physical senses. But in the dream state, you judge and reason and are guided by your finer, more powerful spiritual senses.

Perhaps, in a dream, you are told to beware of going for a swim. Sure enough, you learn that the area you customarily frequent had suddenly developed a dangerous undertow and that the lifeguard on duty, in effecting a rescue, was very nearly drowned in the process.

Precognition—the ability of foreseeing the future—is a familiar experience, especially to women with their acute sense of intuition.

The story is told of a woman who dreamed

that she was driving to Texas with her husband. They were speeding along on the highway when she saw a car come at them from a blind driveway at the right. Her husband swerved left, preventing a broadside collision.

She awoke, somewhat shaken, and related the dream to him. He shrugged the whole thing off as being nothing more than a dream, since he had no intention of going to Texas.

However, months later, he found himself behind the wheel, actually driving there to consummate an unexpected deal.

Sure enough, just as his wife had seen it in her dream, a car suddenly appeared from a blind driveway at his right. He recalled her words, swerved sharply, and so avoided a fatal collision.

Such a dream proves that the human mind can leap over the boundaries of reality and come upon an experience far off in the future.

Very often, a dream which depicts a scene about to take place is later matched in every detail when the curtain opens to reveal it in all its reality.

History records that King Croesus, in a dream, saw his son Athys being murdered. Soon after, the deed itself followed the vision. The boy was killed by the man who had been assigned to protect him. It seemed that the finger of fate could not point in any other direction.

A young girl, engaged to be married, had a

hunch that her fiance was misrepresenting his true status.

What troubled her so deeply was the fact that although he appeared to be in love with her, he made no move to set a wedding date. As time went on, he seemed on the brink of broaching the subject yet always withdrew.

The months dragged on. He grew more and more attentive and loving, yet more and more disinclined to be serious in his suit.

The girl was puzzled by his behavior. She sensed there was something wrong. Her parents were annoyed at the protracted engagement. There was still no ring on their daughter's finger and other suitors were waiting in the wings.

Something had to happen. It did.

In response to the girl's prayers, the answer came but from a most unexpected source. She dreamed every scene of the drama!

In her dream, she saw a woman come to the door with an infant in her arms. The woman explained that the girl might expect no marriage since she was the rightful wife and this infant was the rightful offspring of the man who was presently paying court.

Was this only a vision?

Was there any truth to the dream?

The girl determined to have a heart-to-heart talk with her fiance and get to the bottom of the situation.

The next evening, while they were driving

through the countryside on their way to the
home of a friend, she appeared more silent
than usual. The apparition of the wife still
haunted her.

Finally he asked her what was wrong. She
told him. She added there was no doubt it was
nothing more or less than a crazy dream.

It was then he told her that it was far from
crazy. It was only too true. He did have a wife
from whom he was divorced. He did have a
son—just as she had envisioned. That was the
reason he had been so reluctant to ask her to
marry him. But now that she knew the truth,
would she be his wife and set the wedding day?

Now, what had brought on such a dream?

What was the underlying cause?

Was it an answer to prayer?

Had her subconscious mind responded to
her need?

Had his subconscious mind—filled as it was
with guilt and the fear of losing her, finally
crossed the invisible border of sleep and revealed the truth to her in a dream?

The fact remains that the subconscious mind
ranges over a wider expanse in our lives than
the conscious mind with its limitations. The
subconscious has greater insight. This being
the case, it cannot be doubted that foresight
is also one of its attributes and so produces
dreams in which premonition plays a prominent role.

As you know, your conscious mind concentrates on the present. However, when you go to sleep and your conscious mind is relaxed, the subconscious takes over, whether to prophesy, warn or merely recharge your body, tired from its day of work. It is then the subconscious not only serves you in a hundred different ways but also uses the hours of slumber to rest your limbs and restore your heart.

It is then that your subconscious mind, being more powerful than your conscious mind—as hypnotism has shown—reviews whatever has passed through your conscious mind, distilling via your dreams whatever message it finds necessary to impart to you.

There are times you remember your dreams. There are times you cannot recall a single incident. All that you know is the fact that you dreamed.

At times, your dream may have some connection with a condition which calls for attention. You might feel a terrible thirst. You either get up to relieve it by taking a drink— or you gratify it while still dreaming that your thirst has been quenched. Since your wish for a drink of water has been granted to you in your dream— you will keep on sleeping peacefully. It is in this manner that your subconscious makes an effort to serve and protect you while you are asleep instead of waking you up to attend to some need.

You may have indulged in a heavy dinner before retiring and are suffering from a bad case of indigestion which affects the blood circulation as well as the circulation to the brain. This accounts for the subject of your dream in which you find yourself embroiled in an argument or in a tight situation from which you are unable to extricate yourself. Perhaps you are trapped in an elevator or hanging on a building ledge above the street.

You may wake from a dream with a sense of relief when you find yourself safe. On the other hand, you may be weighted down by depression which dampens your spirit for the rest of the day.

You may have suffered a humiliating dream or a terrifying dream which left you apprehensive or even a dream of frustration, the reason you are so irritable.

It is very difficult to evaluate your dream. This requires a knowledge of your nature and temperament. Your surroundings—your friends—your business—your love life—all of it enters into the pattern of interpretation.

Let's say that you dream of fire.

This can mean a happy, peaceful time around the family hearth with those you love. It can also mean that the hidden force of fear has come to the surface of your subconscious mind and you must now face an ugly situation.

Perhaps you experience a sense of flying in your dream.

No two experts agree on the symbol that is shown to you. One will say that a dream of

flying indicates your longing to escape from
your work, your married life, your single status.
The other may interpret the dream of flying as
repression, a turning back to those remote days
when mankind floated without any effort on
the face of the sea.

Dreams come in a variety of visions, including the familiar ones of missing or catching a
train—running away and being caught—walking naked through the streets—or standing at
the bedside of a loved one as he dies.

You may even dream of the long ago of
your childhood with all its nostalgic memories.
This, according to the scientist, is the child who
still sleeps in your adult unconscious and
emerges now and then to intrigue and amuse
you.

The dream may appear to be lengthy, yet
take no more than a very few minutes to experience.

A dream may be very vivid and yet apt to be
forgotten. It is seldom remembered complete in
every detail as you dreamed it. You may remember only snatches of your dreams.

But, according to Hazlitt who preceded
Freud, when you sleep, you are no longer a
hypocrite. You don't have to excuse your
opinions. You don't have to hide your true
feelings. You are now off-guard and enjoying
your new, entirely candid personality!

There are times when the last thought you

take into sleep with you moves into action as a dream.

Sometimes, someone you met during the day leaves so vivid an impression that the individual appears to you as a vision.

Sometimes, the remnant of the thoughts you gather up during your waking hours becomes the sum total of your sleeping hours.

You should learn to listen with avid attention, to whatever is told to you in your dream.

A plumber's wife awoke from a terrible nightmare. She dreamed that she saw her husband installing a pipe line on the job. The operation was fraught with danger. She watched the big iron bucket swinging in and out of place on the big iron pipe. It traveled three times across her vision. The third time that it moved, it broke free from its mooring.

The dream was so vivid that she bolted upright in bed, shook her husband awake and described what had happened.

He promised her faithfully to show the greatest caution on the job and watch the men as well.

Sure enough, a few days later, the giant pipe she had described arrived on the truck along with the bucket. They were swung into place. The chains that were meant to secure them began to give way—and, just as in her dream—on the third swing, the bucket slipped.

Her husband sounded the warning and the crew made for safety in the nick of time, barely

missing the bucket and the pipe as it rocketed
down to earth.

Now what did such a dream prove?

It pointed to the fact that man can travel in
sleep without being bound by either time or
space. Mind can travel here, there, everywhere,
able to warn, guide or conduct the affairs of the
dreamer.

Always give your dream its due.

Never push it to one side as being of no
consequence.

Regard the dream, given birth in your subconscious, as the key that will open the lock
for you to those innumerable sealed doors
which guard the entrance to the Great Within!

Chapter 8

Thou shalt not be afraid; yea, thou shalt lie down, and thy sleep shall be sweet.
—Proverbs 3:24

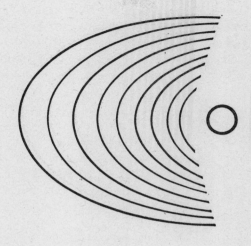

SLEEP IS A VITAL FORCE IN YOUR LIFE.

This has been proven at Walter Reed Hospital and other institutions which have been making extensive studies in the field.

Experiments, depriving people of sleep, have established that the subjects collapsed under pressure. Mirages appeared before their eyes. Reptiles crawled all over them. Cobwebs covered their faces.

Sleep is essential.

It not only rebuilds the body, but it serves to refresh and vitalize the mind.

When you sleep, a cord known as the silver link which connects your body to your spirit, goes out into space. You become two people—the sleeping form on the bed and the spirit that is free on the wing in the ether. You commence to lead two lives.

All sorts of strange things may happen to you. You go off on all sorts of adventures.

You may fly off to visit the race track and be given the winner in a symbol.

A compulsive gambler who believed in signs dreamed of a horse that ran in the rain on a track covered with mud. He bet on the mud horse and he won.

Another race track habitué dreamed that he heard the name Gypsy over the radio. The name took his fancy. But it seemed too far-fetched to accept it as the sign of a winner or so much as remember in relation to the race track.

However, his subconscious mind did not fail to remember this, in spite of the fact that at lunch that day with a friend, he asked if a horse named Gypsy rang a bell. The friend replied there was no such horse scheduled to run. But sure enough, there was a horse named Gypsy and it was Gypsy who won the race.

Dreams reach out to make your fortune for you—or protect you from losing it.

A woman dreamed she went swimming in a clay pit that seemed to have no bottom. She read the writing on the wall. To her, here was a sign that the financial investment the broker recommended would sink in a bottomless pit. Sure enough, the proposition proved to be disastrous and, if not for her ability to interpret her dream, she would have sacrificed every cent of her savings.

Although dreams of warning are prone to come true, you may dream of a fire only to awaken to find that you turned up the current in your electric blanket to an unbearable heat. Your subconscious mind presented your predicament to you in the form of a fire. Perhaps it decided this was a more exciting symbol than waving an ordinary blanket in your face!

Some people keep right on dreaming in spite of the ringing of an alarm clock.

A young photographer who had made quite a reputation for himself, confessed that he owned three alarm clocks, all of which he set to make sure they would ring and wake him up.

Yet he slept on, blissful in spite of their concerted jangle.

However, he arranged for his mother to telephone him every morning at 6 A.M. The third ring of the phone always succeeded in bringing him out of sleep.

He explained that this was no doubt due to the fact that a bond existed between them. Apparently, they tuned in on the same vibration length. She really did not need to telephone her son. She could merely call his name and it would wake him up—as she used to awaken him when he was a boy.

Some people dream in color. The colors are vivid. The features of the faces appear life-like and alert.

Some people dream only in black and white. Some dreams—to some people appear as a jumbled mass, difficult to distinguish.

It is claimed that dreams which come in color are more than just dreams. They may be an out-of-the-body experience such as takes place in astral trance.

Many instances of those who have projected themselves spiritually come under this category.

People who have met with automobile accidents have attested to seeing their bodies lying on the ground while they are floating in horizontal fashion directly over them. They are able to see themselves as apart from themselves, breathing yet unconscious.

Records reveal that in 1876, Sir William Barrett read a paper in which he described astral travel.

The subject projected the mind to a distant place and returned with the report of what was transpiring there. It also furnished an extensive description of the area, its terrain, homes and peoples.

Of course, the public regarded any such happenstance as being purely ridiculous, a fanciful concoction, conceived by Sir William in an unguarded moment.

How could a body separate itself from its soul unless death cut the bond between them?

It is true that under anaesthesia or drugs or when a subject lies in a coma, there is a separation between the physical body and the spiritual self. As a result, there may be little or no memories retained of the experience itself.

However, it has been proven that people do travel during sleep. They respond to astral projection particularly when under hypnosis, the spirit leaving the body and taking to space.

Hypnosis, a close kin to sleep, can be put to good use, particularly in the training of a child.

An expert can cure stammering in children, bedwetting, masturbation and sleepwalking. The child may be a liar, a thief, a poor student in school, a problem in the home.

The method is simple. You stand at the bedside of the sleeping child.

Use a gentle tone. Tell the child that the speaker is about to address it. Tell it that it will hear every word but that the words will not disturb it nor wake it up.

Then feed it the necessary suggestions in simple sentences, repeating each one several times.

The child rarely awakens. If it does, it

usually drops off to sleep again and the session can be continued.

Of course, it may not respond immediately to the treatment but repeated sessions are sure to produce rewarding results.

Be sure that the child is relaxed, that the room is quiet and conducive to sleep. The child should be in a comfortable bed in an easy position. Its arms and legs should not be hanging over the bed or brought up to its chest in a huddle. Its eyes should be closed without the lids fluttering and its mouth should not be open.

In the olden days, a child was warned not to sleep with an open mouth. Otherwise, the soul could fly out between the lips and leave the body forever.

The practice of hypnotism—along with auto-suggestion can benefit you as well as your child.

It is important that you do a thorough job of housecleaning your mind before dropping off to sleep.

Talk to your subconscious as if it were your counsellor.

Always designate the pattern of your activities for the following day.

Impress your subconscious with a pattern and it will work in that direction all night long while you are asleep.

All mankind knows the importance of sleeping on a difficult problem. There is a proverb which states that sleep brings wisdom.

Practice sleeping on a difficult problem before you make a definite decision especially when you give the subconscious proper directions first. The subconscious can think things over more completely during sleep than during the waking state.

Always take steps to counteract an undesirable dream by impressing desirable conditions upon the subconscious.

Dreams of good should be encouraged. This can be done by directing the subconscious to work toward the promotion of good in your life.

In fact, a good dream is actually a prophecy indicating what the subconscious can do, is ready to do, or is about to do. This prophecy can be made to come true by your determination and your faith.

It is a good thing to jot down your dream immediately upon awakening so that you can still capture the spoils extended to you by your sleeping senses before your waking senses enter into the picture and confiscate your catch.

When you tell a dream—either to yourself or to someone else—do not color it with segments of imagination or you will lose the true significance of what your subconscious mind is attempting to impart to you—or solve for you.

Always balance negative dreams by positive

dreams in which you inherit huge sums of money, stand up to your wife or the world or whoever you need to face fearlessly.

See yourself successful and prosperous and acclaimed.

If you apply these simple rules, you will be surprised at the results.

Make no mistake about it!

The subconscious listens!

The subconscious hears!

The subconscious achieves!

Chapter 9

Commune with your own heart upon your bed, and be still.

—Psalms 4:4

THE ENGLISH WORD HYPNOTISM HAS ITS DER-
ivation in the Greek word meaning sleep.

Webster's defines it as "A temporary normal
suspension of consciousness occurring periodi-
cally."

It defines dreaming as "A succession of
pictures of mental images received in sleep
which are apt to be fantastic."

Other reference works label sleep as a state

of trance or some degree of insensibility to surroundings.

According to Hazlitt and Descartes who were scientists of the early school that dealt with the mind, mankind dreamed all night, remembering only fragments of that which took place yet the mind was always alert even when in sleep.

Both doctors and hypnotists have been known to induce sleep in order to remove fear, anger, violence, a disposition to lie or loot as well as to correct stammering and improve speech.

Russian scientists have done extensive research in the field of dreams. According to their experts, dreams in the form of flood, famine, battlefield scenes, drownings, especially in muddy waters, and other such crises warn the dreamer of approaching illness.

Both illness and accidents are often anticipated in dreams.

Death may also appear in a vision.

A dream may be due to a repressed emotion of one sort or another.

Dreams assume various patterns.

They can be vivid, coherent and intelligible. They can also be misty, vague and visionary.

It is a simple matter for some people to remember every detail of a dream, recalling it like the scenes in a play in the exact continuity in which it made its appearance onstage.

At other times, you may dream incoherently

in segments which float like broken clouds before your eyes, making neither rhyme nor reason. All you know is that you dreamed. You remember very little and that little makes little sense.

Some dreams come in color. These may be either very vivid or quite subdued in tone.

Other dreams are depicted in black and white. Your dream can vary in length.

It may take only a few seconds, yet last as long as an hour. The average dreamer may dream for two hours, yet not remember any of it upon awakening.

It has developed that the longer you sleep following a dream, the less you are apt to remember your dream. Numerous tests have proven that those who awoke five minutes following a dream usually had better recall than those who awoke fifteen minutes after the dreaming period came to an end.

Extensive experiments have been launched at the William C. Menninger Dream Laboratory in the psychiatric department of the Maimonides Hospital in Brooklyn in order to ascertain whether or not dreams can be induced telepathically.

Volunteers sleep overnight in various laboratories assigned to them. Then research workers stationed at some distance away, transmit thoughts or images to the sleepers who are awakened every few moments and checked as to the dreams which appeared to them.

According to Sigmund Freud, the famous physician who was born in 1856, the most prominent underlying motive of a dream was some wish on the part of the dreamer. He maintained that dreams either sheathed the ego or revealed a selfish motive. He accented the sexual drive in man. In his estimation, the sexual motive—in whatever form—constituted the prominent feature, the desire for sex being even stronger than the longing for food, air or water. To dream of an object such as a snake, a knife or a sword representing the male sex organ was to experience sex vicariously. A room, an opening, a box or any symbol which resembled a container, represented the female organ. This, in a dream, spoke plainly to Freud.

In his estimation, Freud attributed such visions in his patients while in the sleep state to a deep craving for love. The process of psychoanalysis—as he practiced it—was to uncover the unconscious wish of the patient and through this means, make the required correction.

He recommended dreaming to his patients, for in this way, he assured them that the conscious wish was often realized.

He believed it of utmost importance, to analyze dreams. According to Freud, analysis helped to relieve tension, illness and nervous breakdown. His method was to take the dream apart, piece by piece and trace it back to its inception.

A child, for instance, could hate its own parent.

In the case of a girl, its affection was directed to the father. In the case of a boy, love went out to the mother. The child experienced repulsion, jealousy and dislike for the parent which happened to have the same sex.

Freud was of the conviction that nervous tensions were the result of repression. He labeled this as the Oedipus Complex, taking the name from King Oedipus of Thebes who married his own mother without knowing who she was and as a result, lost his life for the questionable deed.

On the other hand, Jung, who was Freud's student at one time, established his own theory.

Although Jung agreed with many of Freud's interpretations, he maintained that dreams were a form of symbol, presented to the dreamer for the purpose of guidance. Jung put the sexual dream—which Freud considered so important—in its proper place. No. Dreams were not the desire to fulfill an unrequited wish for love. They were the means given to man to adjust his life. Freud might look to cure the ills of the past in a subject. Jung's objective was to prevent the ills from occurring in the future.

Further research on his part produced further revelations.

Jung discovered that his patients were reluctant to answer the questions that he posed to them. So he presented them with a word test by which he could ascertain proper treatment. In this manner, he could put his finger on those incidents which were painful to his clients as well as uncover the innermost secrets. What, he would ask, did a certain word mean?

At times, the replies made little sense. The patient thought this method was meaningless. But Jung thought otherwise. More often than not, the connotation revealed a subterranean river flowing deep below the surface of the person.

Neither Freud nor Jung were the only researchers on the scene of sleep.

Havelock Ellis, the celebrated authority, advanced still another theory.

In his works on the subject, he declared that dreams emanated entirely from man's inner being. It was man's emotions that brought color to his dreams. Dreams came, brought either on the wings of thought or some remembered image of the past. Perhaps, at the instant of falling asleep, the body was subject to some sort of physical stimulation.

This theory was echoed in part by Jack London, the author, who advanced the idea that when you dream you are naked, you are merely reverting back to the time of the cavemen, when nudity was not regarded as shameful. He also explained that the reason for falling in a dream was because lying outstretched in bed contrasted with being on your feet in a walking, or upright position.

The dream of falling has still another explanation, having its origin in the prehistoric man who lived in a tree and met his death by dropping to the ground. Still another theory is that lying down goes against the pull of the earth's gravity.

At times, dreams owe their source to the physical well-being or discomfort of the subject.

You dream you are naked. This may be due to the fact that the blanket may have slipped from your body.

As a rule, your dream is visual. You may seem to speak, but you hear no sound. You may fire a gun. You meet with silence. Even when you drive a car, there is no purr from the engine, no voices are audible, coming to you from those on the street. You see only their faces, clearly or otherwise.

Professor W. S. Monroe made a study of three hundred dreams of fifty-five of the women students of Westfield Normal School in Massachusetts.

His findings were as follows:

Taste impressions in fewer than one percent of the dreams:
Smell impressions in more than one percent.
Movement impressions in five percent.

Touch impressions in three percent.
Hearing impressions in twenty-six percent.
Sight impressions in sixty-seven percent.

Bergson came forward with still another theory. He declared that the dream presented the actual life of the dreamer with some of its anxieties, worries, tensions and failings invoked by sleep.

According to Bergson, the waking hours of man are spent in the atmosphere of the present. In dreams, it is merged with the past. Thought mingles with thought, each one battling the other for the opportunity to rise and make itself apparent.

Dr. Kleitman, of the University of Chicago, who has been studying sleep, ably assisted by Dr. William Dement, has found that up-and-down eye movements are connected with dreams of climbing while side-to-side movements indicate horizontal activities experienced in dreaming.

They have also discovered that prior to the beginning of a dream, the sleeper twists and turns or moves his arms and legs. However, once the dream is in motion, the subject quiets down and only minor movements such as the twitching of fingers are noticeable. The dream ends with the dreamer again twisting or moving his limbs. Also, while dreaming, the body temperature may go as high as ninety-nine degrees Fahrenheit and still remain normal.

Adler, the psychologist, introduced the inferiority complex which enjoyed a great vogue at the time.

He originated the idea of the wish-fulfillment, the desire for power, acting as a form of compensation to combat the feeling of inferiority in the individual.

Adler's psychology with its accent on power, contrasted sharply with the psychoanalysis as presented by Freud and the analytical psychology which Jung claimed gave expression in man.

Investigators agree that there is a great deal of overlap between night dreams, hypnotic dreams and dreams in trance such as experienced by Edgar Cayce who discovered himself in his dreams.

Many of Cayce's dreams were prophetic.

He dreamed he would be married. The marriage took place.

He dreamed of his death, as well as the death of his wife.

He gave almost thirty thousand readings, received in a state of sleep. In fact, he became known as the sleeping doctor.

The method he employed was to go into total amnesia. He had no control over the statements he made while he slept. In fact, upon awakening, he did not remember all he had said and had to be told what the reading contained.

His method was uniquely his own.

The person requiring help could either be present or off at a great distance.

Cayce would become slightly pink around the chest and throat, then turn red, as if gathering power to move out of his body in order to read the condition that needed to be healed. Then, while still in sleep, he would recommend certain drugs, various exercises, or whatever the patient required to bring about the healing.

He spoke like a doctor using medical terminology. His medical examinations were thorough and almost always accurate.

Cayce felt that dreams were replete with symbols. A gorilla represented man's lower animal nature. The sight of a madman represented unrestrained anger. A ship's captain represented a steady helmsman or the higher self. A house where one once lived might relate to a traumatic occurrence experienced on the premises. A rough road represented harsh travails.

His work received wide acclaim. The Edgar Cayce Foundation has been established at Virginia Beach as a tribute to his theory that the world of dreams can be more revealing than the world of reality.

The search for the key to the dream keeps turning in the lock of a door still closed to mankind.

In 1950, the electroencephalograph was introduced.

Electrodes were used to mark the various

levels of sleep, the length of dreams, the effect upon the sleeper when deprived of sleep. There have also been experiments involving the recall of dreams, sleepwalking, and the impact of ESP upon the dreamer.

Today, the study of dreams is being pursued on many levels, seeking its way out of the consulting room where so often it was locked behind doors of secrecy and brought out into the open with an invitation to the inquiring mind.

Yet great as we acknowledge the contributions of scientific mind, even Science continues to be baffled by what happens to man during sleep.

We have still to find the answer.

Chapter 10

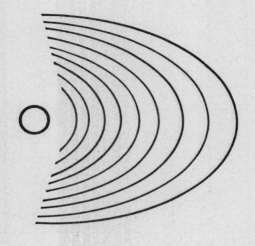

I laid me down and slept; I awaked; for the Lord sustained me.

—Psalms 3:5

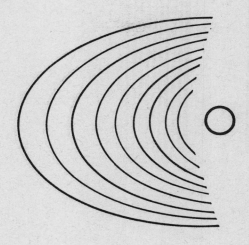

THE BIBLE IS RICH IN DREAMS.

The psalmists laid claim to the fact that God spoke to them through dreams. According to them, the truth bears witness as it sings in the ethereal beauty and the exquisite, memorable language of those psalms.

Who can voice the Twenty-third or the Ninety-first Psalm without an overwhelming sense of the spirit, rising like a fountain from within—to inspire, illumine and refresh?

Who can pray, with the language of the Bible like a banister of support for the uncertain hand—without finding strength of heart and avenue of purpose?

There is the mark of the dreamer in the Psalms, mystical, powerful, and beautiful. Small wonder the psalmist made certain to record them.

The prophets were also moved to speak in the tongue of prophesies.

What else were dreams but the speech of the night when the world was silent and the senses slumbered?

It was then man could listen with his inner being to the dream which came to him, serving as a vital function in his life.

Dreams, said the mystic, were barbed with a hundred arrows, each shot into space with an aim that was certain and true. Each served its own peculiar purpose.

Some dreams were messages from God, veiled with warning. Others were instructions to be studied and obeyed. Still others pointed to the fortunes—or misfortunes—of the future. Dreams were the pillow for the night of sleep, like a book to be read by the soul of the sleeper.

Saint and seer—king and common man—all believed in the great potency contained in dreams, some of which were hidden while others were revealed, the meaning made plain by the interpreter.

Such great souls as St. Augustine and St. Hubert were both inspired and influenced by the visions they received from sources they declared to be divine.

The day and age was ripe for the mystic. Occultism flourished. The doorstep of the soothsayer was polished bright by many feet. Great credence was placed upon the art of revelation.

However, there were those among the soothsayers who spoke God's word to all who would listen and yet had no traffic in the popular concept of divining. These were holy men who gave themselves over to constant prayer and deep meditation. Who else could attain to the heights except those deserving of the kinship with Spirit?

Yet, the Bible records numerous instances in which divination is denied to the solicitor even though he may be wealthy, influential and in a position of power as in the case of King Saul who wept when God no longer answered his prayers either through dreams or by prophets.

As a rule, the prophet or diviner, particularly among the Jews, was apt to be a man. But women diviners were also consulted and held in high esteem.

The people set great store in their findings, in spite of Jeremiah whose wrath was provoked by a populace which sought out soothsayers. Jeremiah exhorted the masses to lay aside their foolishness. He counseled them not to listen.

In Jeremiah 27:9-10 as recorded in the Bible he declared:

> *Therefore harken not ye to your prophets, nor to your diviners, nor to your dreamers, nor to your enchanters, nor to your sorcerers, which speak unto you saying, Ye shall not serve the King of Babylon:*

> *For they prophesy a lie unto you, to remove you far from your land; and that I should drive you out, and ye should perish.*

The people, however, persisted in consulting the diviner, for it was in divining, they firmly believed, that they read the direction their lives were to take or toward the hidden reason of what had happened.

The period was a colorful one and steeped in superstition. At the time—even as today—dreams were a way of life.

It was the custom of the royal court to maintain seers. They regarded their tellers of fortune with due reverence and delegated them to high office in the kingdom.

According to the religious scholar of the

day, dreams were believed to have their origin in the realm of the supernatural. Visions were read in the light of symbols, appearing during slumber in order to foretell the future or bring forth the destiny of man.

Occult science and astrology were subjects of endless discourse. Voluminous text that filled innumerable dream books which sold in vast quantities and enjoyed a tremendous vogue.

Both New and Old Testaments are replete with the dramatic accounts of dreamers and their dreams, messages, prophesies, counseling and divination.

Dreams, spelling trouble and ill-fortune by far exceed those of rejoicing and good fortune.

The words of the seer sound out stern and ominous. The words of warning toll out a sober message to both rich and poor.

Pontius Pilate, for instance, was beseeched by his wife to turn away from his act of evil which she envisioned—or dire consequences would follow. Her dream, as you know, came to pass.

The Holy Family was told to turn aside into Egypt.

In Genesis, a deep sleep fell upon Adam, and out of this sleep, Eve, the mother of men was born.

Zechariah, the son of the prophet Iddo (Zechariah 1-7) received the word of God as the result of a vision.

The dreams and the visions which came to the consecrated, were usually preceded by long vigils given over to fasting and prayer. Many an Apostle was converted in this manner.

The Jews, in particular, were firm believers in the messages they received from their seers who often retreated into the hills and caves for protracted periods of contemplation and prayers, and emerged with messages, which they declared, came to them direct from the fountainhead. The Jews maintained that in times of need, angels came to them as direct messengers, sent by God, bearing words of counsel, warning or guidance.

Guidance—through dreams, was an accepted fact both in the Hebraic and pagan worlds.

Israel was of the firm conviction that God made His will known to His chosen ones, using the person of the Diviner as His holy instrument.

In Genesis 28:11-16, it reads:

> *And he lighted upon a certain place, and tarried there all night, because the sun was set; and he took of the stones of that place and put them for his pillows and lay down in that place to sleep.*

> *And he dreamed, and behold a ladder set up on the earth, and the top of it*

reached to heaven; and behold the angels of God ascending and descending on it.

And behold, the Lord stood above it, and said I am the Lord God of Abraham thy father, and the God of Isaac: the land whereon thou liest, to thee will I give it, and to thy seed.

And thy seed shall be as the dust of the earth, and thou shalt spread abroad to the west, and to the east, and to the north, and to the south: and in thee and in thy seed shall all the families of the earth be blessed.

And, behold, I am with thee, and will keep thee in all places whither thou goest, and will bring thee again into this land; for I will not leave thee, until I have done that which I have spoken to thee of.

And Jacob awaked out of his sleep, and he said, Surely the Lord is in this place; and I knew it not.

The promise contained in the dream appeared crystal clear to Jacob, becoming manifested in time.

Jacob had numerous dreams. He endowed the angels on the ladder reaching to Heaven with psychic as well as spiritual meaning.

Laban, the uncle and father-in-law to Jacob also dreamed. Laban heard the voice of God warning him not to harm Jacob.

It was through the channel of dreams that God was shown to exist to the Jews, for, in the Old Testament, the words said to be direct from Heaven, declared to Moses:

> *"If there be a prophet among you, I, the Lord, will make myself known to him in a vision and will speak to him in a dream."*

God, in all the reality of a living Presence— promised to abide with such as Jacob and his people throughout eternity.

In fact, it was through the means of a dream that Jacob was given the idea of tithing—a practice which has since come down to us to this day. Tithing—the sharing of a portion of one's earnings or possessions—is regarded by the faithful as a sure way of inducing the increase of prosperity. It calls for the giving of one-tenth, if not more, and promises to increase by tenfold.

The prospect of tithing with its certain reward which appeared to Jacob in a dream, was matched by his promise to willingly tithe forevermore all his possessions if God would take care of his needs and guide him and his people.

Jacob dreamed often and long.

He related his dreams, firm in the belief that

they were prophesies, presaging great good. He claimed that God—by way of angels, came to him in a vision, counseling him to rise and return to the land of his kin.

Another account of a dream and its dreamer is told in the story of Joseph, a familiar one to those who read the Bible.

No doubt you know Joseph's history as it is related in Genesis 37:5-11. The Bible states:

And Joseph dreamed a dream, and he told it his brethren: and they hated him yet the more.

And he said unto them, Hear, I pray you, this dream which I have dreamed:

For, behold, we were binding sheaves in the field, and, lo, my sheaf arose and also stood upright, and, behold, your sheaves stood round about, and made obeisance to my sheaf.

And his brethren said to him, Shalt thou indeed reign over us? Or shalt thou indeed have dominion over us? And they hated him yet the more for his dreams, and for his words.

And he dreamed yet another dream, and told it his brethren, and said, Behold, I have dreamed a dream more; and, be-

hold, the sun and the moon and the eleven stars made obeisance to me.

And he told it to his father, and to his brethren: and his father rebuked him, and said unto him, What is this dream that thou has dreamed? Shall I and thy mother and thy brethren indeed come to bow down ourselves to thee to the earth?

And his brethren envied him; but his father observed the saying.

According to the Bible, it was Joseph's dream which propelled all that transpired in his life—from beginning to end, the drama of his desertion by his brothers, his capture by the Egyptians, his years of bondage.

And, surely you know the rest of that story —his days at court and in jail—his recall to court in order to read Pharaoh's dream.

The King assumed—as did his people—that a King's dream was of divine origin—just as during the Middle Ages, Joan of Arc who was conceded to be one of the most revered dreamers in all history.

However, Joseph refuted Pharaoh and his belief in his divinity. He insisted that interpretation—as well as the original vision—came alone from God. He saw the seven good kine in the dream as seven years of plenty. He saw the seven lean kine as seven years of famine.

And thus it came to pass, a dream made true in the time that followed when he was made second in command to Pharaoh.

His father Jacob was also moved by a vision. It appeared in a dream, instructing him to send his sons to Joseph and ask for grain during the years of famine.

Scholars of the Bible regard the dreams of Joseph and Daniel as the most notable dreams in the Old Testament.

The Books of Daniel are based on dreams. It is stated in Daniel 2:1-19, 25-29 and 47-48:

And in the second year of the reign of Nebuchadnezzar Nebuchadnezzar dreamed dreams, wherewith his spirit was troubled, and his sleep brake from him.

Then the king commanded to call the magicians, and the astrologers, and the sorcerers, and the Chaldeans, for to shew the king his dreams. So they came and stood before the king.

And the king said unto them, I have dreamed a dream, and my spirit was troubled to know the dream.

Then spake the Chaldeans to the king in Syriack, O king, live for ever: tell thy servants the dream, and we will shew the interpretation.

The king answered and said to the Chaldeans, The thing is gone from me: if ye will not make known unto me the dream, with the interpretation thereof, ye shall be cut in pieces, and your houses shall be made a dunghill.

But if ye shew the dream, and the interpretation thereof, ye shall receive of me gifts and rewards and great honour: therefore shew me the dream, and the interpretation thereof.

They answered again and said, Let the king tell his servants the dream, and we will shew the interpretation of it.

The king answered and said, I know of certainty that ye would gain the time, because ye see the thing is gone from me.

But if ye will not make known unto me the dream, there is but one decree for you: for ye have prepared lying and corrupt words to speak before me, till the time be changed: therefore tell me the dream, and I shall know that ye can shew me the interpretation thereof.

The Chaldeans answered before the king, and said, There is not a man upon the earth that can shew the king's matter: therefore there is no king, lord, nor ruler, that asked such things at any magician, or astrologer, or Chaldean.

And it is a rare thing that the king requireth, and there is none other that can shew it before the king, except the gods, whose dwelling is not with flesh.

For this cause the king was angry and very furious, and commanded to destroy all the wise men of Babylon.

And the decree went forth that the wise men should be slain; and they sought Daniel and his fellows to be slain.

Then Daniel answered with counsel and wisdom to Arioch the captain of the king's guard, which was gone forth to slay the wise men of Babylon.

He answered and said to Arioch the king's captain, Why is the decree so hasty from the king? Then Arioch made the thing known to Daniel.

Then Daniel went in, and desired of the king that he would give him time, and

*that he would shew the king the inter-
pretation.*

*Then Daniel went to his house, and
made the thing known to Hananiah,
Mishael, and Azariah, his companions:*

*That they would desire mercies of the
God of heaven concerning this secret; that
Daniel and his fellows should not perish
with the rest of the wise men of Babylon.*

*Then was the secret revealed unto
Daniel in a night vision. Then Daniel
blessed the God of heaven.*

*   *   *

*Then Arioch brought in Daniel before
the king in haste, and said unto him, I
have found a man of the captives of
Judah, that will make known unto the
king the interpretation.*

*The king answered and said to Daniel,
whose name was Belteshazzar, Art thou
able to make know unto me the dream
which I have seen, and the interpretation
thereof?*

*Daniel answered in the presence of the
king, and said, The secret which the king*

hath demanded cannot the wise men, the astrologers, the magicians, the soothsayers, shew unto the king;

But there is a God in heaven that revealeth secrets, and maketh known to the king Nebuchadnezzar what shall be in the latter days. Thy dream, and the visions of thy head upon thy bed, are these:

As for thee, O king, thy thoughts came into thy mind upon thy bed, what should come to pass hereafter; and he that revealeth secrets maketh known to thee what shall come to pass.

*   *   *

The king answered unto Daniel and said, Of a truth it is, that your God is the God of gods, and a Lord of kings, and a revealer of secrets, seeing thou couldest reveal this secret.

Then the king made Daniel a great man, and gave him many great gifts, and made him ruler over the whole province of Babylon, and chief of the governors over all the wise men of Babylon.

An old belief, which has long been cherished —is written—in words of wisdom. They say that God speaks sometimes once, sometimes twice, yet man fails to listen. Yet when night comes—in a dream—when deep sleep cradles the sleeper, then God opens the ears of man. He teaches, guides, warns, strengthens and inspires, sending his angels in the form of visions for the dreamer to dream true.

This was the traumatic experience of the Great King Solomon, as recorded in I Kings 3:5-14:

In Gibeon the Lord appeared to Solomon in a dream by night: and God said, Ask what I shall give thee.

And Solomon said, Thou hast shewed unto thy servant David my father great mercy, according as he walked before thee in truth, and in righteousness, and in uprightness of heart with thee; and thou hast kept for him this great kindness, that thou hast given him a son to sit on his throne, as it is this day.

And now, O Lord my God, thou has made thy servant king instead of David my father: and I am but a little child: know not how to go out or come in.

And thy servant is in the midst of thy people which thou hast chosen, a great people, that cannot be numbered nor counted for multitude.

Give therefore thy servant an understanding heart to judge thy people, that I may discern between good and bad: for who is able to judge this thy so great a people?

And the speech pleased the Lord, that Solomon had asked this thing.

And God said unto him, Because thou hast asked this thing, and hast not asked for thyself long life; neither hast asked riches for thyself, nor hast asked the life of thine enemies; but hast asked for thyself understanding to discern judgment;

Behold, I have done accordingly to thy words; lo, I have given thee a wise and an understanding heart; so that there was none like thee before thee, neither after thee shall any arise like unto thee.

And I have also given thee that which thou has not asked, both riches, and honour: so that there shall not be any among the kings like unto thee all thy days.

And if thou wilt walk in my ways, to keep my statutes and my commandments,

*as thy father David did walk, then I will
lengthen thy days.*

There were many others who communicated
with God in their dreams.

The experience of Abimelech is recorded in
the Bible in Genesis 20:3-7 accordingly:

> *But God came to Abimelech in a
> dream by night, and said to him, Behold
> thou art but a dead man, for the woman
> which thou has taken; for she is a man's
> wife.*

> *But Abimelech had not come near her:
> and he said, Lord, wilt thou slay also a
> righteous nation?*

> *Said he not unto me, She is my sister?
> and she, even she herself said, He is my
> brother: in the integrity of my heart and
> innocency of my hands have I done this.*

> *And God said unto him in a dream,
> Yea, I know that thou didst this in the
> integrity of thy heart; for I also withheld
> thee from sinning against me: therefore
> suffered I thee not to touch her.*

> *Now therefore restore the man his wife;
> for he is a prophet, and he shall pray for
> thee, and thou shalt live; and if thou re-*

store her not, know thou that thou shalt
surely die, thou and all that are thine.

In the gospel of St. Matthew, the birth of
Jesus is divined in a dream, recorded in Matthew 1:18-25 as follows:

Now the birth of Jesus Christ was on
this wise: When as his mother Mary was
espoused to Joseph, before they came together, she was found with child of the
Holy Ghost.

Then Joseph her husband, being a just
man, and not willing to make her a pub-
lick example, was minded to put her away
privily.

But while he thought on these things,
behold, the angel of the Lord appeared
unto him in a dream, saying, Joseph, thou
son of David, fear not to take unto thee
Mary thy wife; for that which is conceived
in her is of the Holy Ghost.

And she shall bring forth a son, and
thou shalt call his name Jesus: for he shall
save his people from their sins.

Now all this was done, that it might be
fulfilled which was spoken of the Lord by
the prophet, saying,

Behold, a virgin shall be with child, and shall bring forth a son, and they shall call his name Emmanuel, which being interpreted is, God with us.

Then Joseph being raised from sleep did as the angel of the Lord had bidden him and took unto him his wife:

And he knew her not till she had brought forth her firstborn son; and he called his name Jesus.

In a dream, as related in Matthew 2:13, it is told:

And when they were departed, behold, the angel of the Lord appeareth to Joseph in a dream, saying, Arise and take the young child and his mother, and flee into Egypt, and be thou there until I bring thee word: for Herod will seek the young child to destroy him.

And, yet, again in Matthew 2:19-23, it is told:

But when Herod was dead, behold, an angel of the Lord appeareth in a dream to Joseph in Egypt.

Saying, arise, and take the young child and his mother, and go into the land of

Israel: for they are dead which sought the young child's life.

And he arose, and took the young child and his mother, and came into the land of Israel.

But when he heard that Archelaus did reign in Judea in the room of his father Herod, he was afraid to go thither: notwithstanding, being warned of God in a dream, he turned aside into the parts of Galilee:

And he came and dwelt in a city called Nazareth: that it might be fulfilled which was spoken by the prophets, He shall be called a Nazarene.

So spoke the prophets, the soothsayers, the magicians, the seers, the psalmists and the diviners—in the pages of the Bible—as they continue to speak among us in order for us to read the truth about dreams—to this day!